THE OTHER SIDE
OF HISTORY

THE OTHER SIDE OF HISTORY

*An anecdotal reflection on
political transition in South Africa*

Frederik van Zyl Slabbert

JONATHAN BALL PUBLISHERS
JOHANNESBURG & CAPE TOWN

Published in 2006 in paperback by
JONATHAN BALL PUBLISHERS (PTY) LTD
PO Box 33977
Jeppestown
2043

ISBN 186842 250 X

Reprinted three times in 2006

Cover design by
Triple M Design & Advertising
Reproduction and typesetting of text by
Alinea Studio, Cape Town
Set in 11 on 13.5 pt Bembo
Printed and bound by CTP Book Printers, Cape

CONTENTS

ACKNOWLEDGEMENTS

I am sixty-six and am too old to remember all the great friends and colleagues who helped shape my thinking. Whoever you are and wherever you are, thank you and do not feel compromised by the outcome.

To Jenny Nothard, again, thank you for the meticulous preparation of the manuscript. It was done with your usual good grace, patience and dedication.

To Jonathan Ball, my publisher: here we go again, and thank you.

F van Zyl Slabbert
April 2006

I, TOO, AM AN AFRICAN –
IF NOT, WHY NOT?

On 8 May 1996 Deputy President Thabo Mbeki made an acceptance speech on behalf of the ANC when the South African Constitution Bill was accepted by the Constitutional Assembly. It is an evocative, moving and inspirational speech. He defines his Africanness in an inclusive manner, in which I, as a White South African, am unequivocally accepted as an African. So, too, the Coloureds and Indians. For example:

- 'I owe my being to the Khoi and San.'
- 'I am formed of the migrants who left Europe to find a new home on our native land.'
- 'In my veins courses the blood of the Malay slaves who came from the East.'
- 'I am the grandchild who lays fresh flowers on the Boer graves at St Helena and the Bahamas.'
- 'I come of those who were transported from India and China.'
- 'Being a part of all these people, and in the knowledge that none dare contest that assertion, I shall claim that – I am African.'

And then the unambiguous, inclusive statement:

> 'The Constitution whose adoption we celebrate constitutes an unequivocal statement that we refuse to accept that our Africanness shall be defined by our race, colour, gender or historical origins.'

I still have a deep unease, even aversion, to attempts to give ideological, value-laden content to concepts of nationality, ethnicity or race. Perhaps it is because I had an overdose of this growing up in a predominantly rural Afrikaner environment. I will never forget as a 16-year-old on a school visit to the Cango Caves, the lights being dimmed, organ music filling the darkness, and a deep voice announcing: 'Civilisation came to South Africa with the landing of Jan van Riebeeck on 6 April 1652.' Even then I thought: 'How completely and utterly absurd.' There was later at Stellenbosch a dear old professor called Bun Booyens who said: 'An Afrikaner is someone who, when the sun goes down, in his soul hears the tinkling of milk cans and the cooing of doves.' The fact that 'the Afrikaners' were ±80% urbanised when he said this was of little consequence.

I can live with most of the rhetorical and metaphorical flourishes in Thabo Mbeki's 'I am an African' speech because he demystifies the identity of an African by referring to the Constitution that was adopted at the occasion, i.e. Coloureds, Asians, Whites, and the offspring of all the indigenous tribes, are all African. Personally, I am happy to give the concept 'African' an unambiguous geographical reference. I am an African because I can trace my history here, and have a South African passport which states that I come from South Africa and am a South African citizen. Apparently the first Slabbert put foot on shore here in 1670. I had absolutely nothing to do with it. One of them had three children with a slave woman. Again, through no fault on my part.

Unfortunately, Mbeki's first inclusive and generous definition of Africanness, almost ten years later, has been ideologically mangled and historically appropriated beyond recognition. The new historiography, often more by implication than by being explicit, makes it quite clear that a Coloured, Indian or White can never be an African. In the South African context, an African, for purposes of policy, is 'a Black of a special kind'. For example, the Broad Based Black Economic Empowerment Act defines a Black as a Coloured, Indian and African. So it is possible to be Black without being African. This is reinforced by the paper on 'the National Question' in *Umrabulo* no. 23 put before the ANC National Congress in June 2005, where it states that the National Question, inter alia, is about 'the liberation of Blacks in general and *Africans in particular*'. Of course, this should offend Mbeki's sense of constitutionality of Africanness as he motivates it in his speech 'I am an African'. Unfortunately, since then, he has increasingly played the 'race card' in considering problems of development and foreign relations: 'Whites think Africans can't govern, Whites think Africans are promiscuous', and so on.

The book on President Thabo Mbeki's speeches, *Africa: Define Yourself*, edited by Essop Pahad and Willie Esterhuyse, never seriously addresses the challenge that he

3

issues. The moment one moves away from using the words 'Africa' and 'African' as uncomplicated geographic references, one enters a world of value-laden and ideological agendas in which one's arguments can regress to a situation in which one looks up the orifices of one's own assumptions, i.e. a tautological quagmire: 'Why am I an African?' 'Because I smell the world in a special way.' 'Why do I smell the world in a special way?' 'Because I am an African.' But the same style and abstraction can be used to give mystical and poetic content to being an Appalachian, Catalonian, Basque, Patagonian, etc. Even an Afrikaner. Ask Oom Bun Booyens about 'the tinkle of the milk cans'.

One of the ANC intellectual heavyweights who excels in this kind of identity mysticism is Pallo Jordan. In a paper delivered at the South African Union Diaspora Conference in Jamaica, 17 March 2005 (also included in *Umrabulo* no. 23), his title is 'Blood is Thicker than Water – the Relevance of Pan Africanism Today'.

In it he says, 'By demonstrating in practice that the blood that binds the peoples of Africa and the diaspora is thicker than the waters of the Atlantic, the Pan African Movement has demonstrated its relevance in tackling the common challenges of the present.' In it he also makes no bones about the fact that Whites are 'the villains' and 'people of African descent are the heroes'. (Thabo, where are you now that we need you?)

You see, when 'we Whites' arrived here in 1652 we found indigenous African tribes filled with 'ubuntu' sharing grazing land and babysitting one another's children. Our 'White racist' forefathers destroyed all that and incul-

4

cated a culture of greed, militancy, envy and selfishness. Racism is a White invention; Africans are genetically incapable of being racists. Unfortunately, Coloureds and Indians inherited some 'White racism', but Africans are mercifully free of it. You see, they have the right kind of blood. And so on, and so forth, blah–blah–blah.

Enough has been written about the different patterns of colonial conquest and exploitation, whether English, Dutch, Belgian, Portuguese, French, Italian or German, for me not to have to waste time expanding on them. Anyone who reads about the exploits of King Leopold in the 'Belgian' Congo can only be filled with revulsion and disgust, even if one does not have 'African blood' (Adam Hochschild: *King Leopold's Ghost*). But before one gets swept away by the exuberance of these bloody references, let us pause to reflect for a moment. I do not know whether Pallo was present at the Slave House on Goree Island in July 1987, but Thabo and I certainly were. The guide, who was an old paratrooper, started expounding on the history of slavery. By the way, he was a black (African?) Senegalese who fought for the French in World War II.

The old man made it quite clear that there was continuous and enthusiastic collusion between African tribes in providing slaves for export by the Portuguese and Dutch slave traders. 'Ubuntu' seems to have been suspended for a while. And by the way, the slave trade along East Africa, e.g. Mozambique and Zanzibar, did not just happen because a slave trader stood on the beach, fired a gun and 300 slaves came crawling out of the bush. They were delivered, manacled and shackled, by men of 'African blood'.

There is a whole new literature reconstructing and re-investigating the history of slavery, including many documentaries written and made by people of 'African blood'. For example, when Alex Haley was challenged on the historical accuracy of his work *Roots*, he said: 'I tried to give my people a myth to live by.' In the same work from which this reference comes (*Black Rednecks and White Liberals*), he says: 'While slavery was common to all civilisations, as well as to people considered to be uncivilised; only one civilisation developed a moral revulsion against it, very late in its history – Western Civilisation. Today, slavery still exists in Mauritania, the Sudan, parts of Nigeria and Benin' (p. 116). He continues: 'Contrary to the "myths to live by" created by Alex Haley and others, Africans were no way the innocents portrayed by *Roots*, baffled as to why White men were coming in and taking their people away in chains. On the contrary, the region of West Africa from which Kunte Kente supposedly came was one of the great slave-trading regions of the continent – before, during and after the White man arrived' (p. 120). (The writer is an African American intellectual, descendant of slaves, and works as a senior research fellow at the Hoover Institute at Stanford University. According to Pallo he must have impeccable African blood!)

The documentary 'The African Trade' (televised on SABC Africa) shows dramatic footage of African Americans breaking down when confronted with evidence of Africans selling fellow Africans into slavery. The slave trade on Goree Island was managed by African women married to slave traders. (I can already anticipate the howls of rage and blasphemous indignation in even mentioning these thoughts. It is like a Palestinian challenging Jewish historiography, and vice versa. They need to define each other out of history in order to capture the future.)

Sowell says of WEB du Bois, whom he admires as much as Pallo Jordan does, that he said of the White New Englanders who established schools in the South after the civil war to educate liberated slaves that it 'was the finest thing in American history'. He continues, 'A wholly disproportionate share of future Black leaders came out of schools and colleges established by New Englanders in the South, not even counting Oberlin College or Dunbar High School. These alumni of institutions founded as New England enclaves in the South included WEB du Bois, James Weldon, Johnson, Langston Hughes, Walter White, Mary McLeod Bethriene, A Phillip Randolph, James Farmer, Thurgood Marshall and Martin Luther King Jnr' (p. 40). He goes on to make the (for Pallo, most outrageous) statement that: 'The advance of European imperialism around the world marked the retreat of the slave trade and then of slavery itself' (p. 117). Of course, the flip side of Pallo's African Blood analogy is Dan Roodt, who argues that European blood is thicker than Atlantic water, and that Afrikaners constitute a Euro-centric enclave battling for their place in the southern African sun. All so utterly boring.

However, whether the concept 'African' is used exclusively or inclusively by government does have an immediate impact on policy and shaping the interaction between the different communities. I have already referred to the BBBEE Act and other 'empowerment oddities' on the domestic front. If the president of my country and some of his ministers decide that Joe Slovo, Helen Joseph, Beyers Naudé, Ronnie Kasrils, Trevor Manuel, Kader Asmal and Van Zyl Slabbert have one thing in common, and that is that they are not African because they are White, Coloured or Indian, it is their problem. Personally, I think it is a load of crap. If you make yourself and others hostage to a racist past, you can budget generously for a racist future.

However, it is on the level of foreign policy where things really become convoluted and interesting. In July 2005, South Africa, together with other African states, was lobbying for two permanent seats on the UN Security Council. (The idea has subsequently been put on hold, but, if pursued again, raises fascinating issues.) The idea is that these two seats would rotate between the five regions into which the African Union is divided: southern Africa, East Africa, West Africa, Central Africa and North Africa. Some fascinating conundrums present themselves. (Nigeria has already said South Africa and Egypt are 'too white' and should not qualify. Ho-ho-ho!) Are 'the inter-ests' that the North African states are going to promote on the Security Council the same as those that the East and southern African states wish to promote? Am I to believe that Egypt, Algeria, Tunisia and Morocco are 'African' in the exclusive sense? For example, are Gaddafi from Libya, Mubarak from Egypt, Bouteflika from Algeria and Abdullah Wade from Senegal, Africans in the inclusive sense that Mbeki uses it in his speech 'I am an African', or in the exclusive sense in which the National Question is formulated and the BBBEE Act is legislated? Is a black

Senegalese Muslim, or is the Muslim brotherhood, the Maribu, that permeates West African politics, African first and Muslim second? Are they Africans in the same way a rural Xhosa, Tswana, Zulu, etc. from South Africa is? What does 'African' in that sense mean?

Anyone who has spent time in Dakar high society, and I include President Abdullah Wade and his corrupt son, soon realises that Paris is still the reference point when it comes to style, fashion and intellectual discourse.

What exactly is the coherence and unity of purpose of the African Union? Wole Soyinka, the Nobel Laureate, refers to it as a 'collection of tyrants, dictators and peace-makers' pursuing self-interest. But let's be generous and accept the principles formulated in its founding document, i.e. that the AU wishes to promote democracy, economic development and respect for human rights on the African continent. I certainly think these principles are worthy of support. But am I as a non-African in South Africa excluded from this mandate? If not, in what sense do I suddenly qualify as an African for the purposes of the African Union? If being black is a necessary but not sufficient condition for being African, are Gaddafi, Bouteflika and Mubarak more black than white? If so, how does one tell? They certainly look more white than black to me.

Of course, there is no end to ridiculing the mystifications and philosophical whimsy that relate to the way the word 'African' is made exclusive and special. Personally, I could not be bothered whether I am included in or excluded from such efforts. I use it, as I have explained, in its simple geographic sense. I am from Africa, therefore

African, because I was born, grew up and live in South Africa and have a South African identity document.

However, underpinning all the preceding points is a more fundamental question. Does South Africa, or Africa for that matter, really need a new dominant ideology? Must there be, in Gramscian terms, 'intellectual hegemony' over 'the masses' or 'the people'? Must they have the 'correct understanding' of the 'National Question'?

For most of its existence the ANC has been an ideology-driven movement (I use the concept 'ideology' in the sense in which the philosopher of science Gustav Bergman used it, i.e. 'an ideological statement is a value judgement presented as a statement of fact', e.g. 'African blood'). This was largely because of the influence of the SACP and organised communism in the Soviet Union and Eastern Europe. Even our current president was a member of the Communist Party and served on its Politburo well into the 1980s.

Communism was, of course, the most widespread redemptive secular ideology of the 20th century, and was teleological in its thrust, i.e. guaranteeing an 'inevitable future' which informs the dynamics or 'dialectics' of the present. Because of this, people ('the masses') who belonged to the movement had a clear sense of purpose, because they were on the winning side (e.g. 'the inevitable victory' of the 'working class' over 'capitalist exploitation' by means of a 'national democratic revolution'). That is why 'the leadership' could promise a chicken in every pot when 'that glorious day' became reality.

But then, organised communism collapsed on 9 November 1989 when the Berlin Wall came down. Suddenly there were no chickens and no pots, and the ANC found itself in ideological meltdown. Overnight it became a movement with no discernible dominant ideology. The fact that it then proceeded to negotiate a liberal democracy for political governance and a market economy for economic development and growth is the clearest evidence of this. This was nothing short of 'ideological blasphemy', given the promises of 'the struggle'. It still sends shudders down the spine of orthodox communists like Nzimande and Cronin, although colleagues like Erwin, Radebe, Kasrils, etc. seem to be adjusting quite well in the new environment. (By the way, one should also not forget that apartheid/separate development was also a redemptive ideology. The struggle between the NP and the ANC was also a struggle between competing forms of political, economic and social redemption.)

However, the combination of Mbeki and Joel Netshitenzhe, CEO of GCIS (Government Communication and Information System) remain an enigma to me in the 'new South Africa'. I have great respect for the intelligence of both. They are serious intellectuals, and if one did not know who had written the piece, it would be difficult to recognise the difference in style and logic. Both try constantly to salvage the rhetoric, if not the substance, of the old struggle ideology. Both argue that South Africa should be a 'developmental State' promoting 'a national democratic revolution' that will answer all the aspects of 'the National Question'. What are these aspects? 'Firstly, to liberate Blacks in general and *Africans in particular* (my emphasis). Secondly, it is the struggle to create a non-racist, non-sexist democratic and united South Africa.

11

Thirdly it is the quest for a single united South African nation with a common overriding identity. Fourthly, it is about resolving the antagonistic contradictions between Black and White. And fifthly, it is about combating tribalism, racialism or any other form of ethnic chauvinism' (*Umrabulo*, no. 23 p. 34).

Generally speaking, I have no problem with most of these objectives, that is, if I understand them correctly. These are, however, highly abstract and philosophical concepts, and I have tried to highlight some puzzles I have in operationalising them. When I do, I have more than a sneaking suspicion that Africanism in an *exclusive* sense is fast becoming the new dominant ideology. Another attempt at redemption?

However, this philosophical preoccupation is not exactly the stuff to inspire the loyal or potential supporter. Compared to the abstract nature of 'the developmental State', 'the National Question' and 'the National Democratic Revolution', the language of the Freedom Charter is very specific and concrete: 'The doors of learning shall be opened to all. South Africa belongs to all who live in it, Black and White', etc. If there is demonstrable failure to deliver on these, then no amount of romanticising and mystifying the concept 'African' is going to placate the discontent of ordinary folk. But, both Mbeki and Netshitenzhe know this, and have written and spoken persuasively about these issues. So then, Lenin's question: What is to be done?

In confronting the very serious challenges facing South Africa and the government, I am not pleading for historical amnesia. On the contrary, I am saying that by inventing the past, or co-opting it ideologically, it becomes more difficult to avoid repeating the mistakes and dealing with the problems of the present. You cannot tell the majority of the people that the ANC led 'a glorious and successful revolution in which the apartheid enemy was crushed' and Thabo was 'a foot soldier of the titanic African army, the ANC', while the concrete and practical benefits of such a 'victory' are not apparent to them.

You cannot tell the majority that Africans are going to be at the top of the economic pile when it comes to economic reconstruction, as they see a few becoming exceedingly wealthy while their own position remains largely unchanged.

I conclude: do not let us invent the past or make ourselves and others ideologically hostage to it. The nature of our challenge is too stark and unambiguous: poverty, unemployment, housing, education, health. And yet we are better off than many other countries, not only in Africa, in addressing these challenges. So as an African, I say to my president, a fellow African, both of us from South Africa: 'Let us get on with it. We don't need no fancy talk.'

CHAPTER 1

INVENTING THE PAST
TO SECURE THE FUTURE

One thing the 'old' and the 'new' South Africa have in common is a passion for inventing history. History is not seen as a dispassionate inquiry into what happened, but rather as a part of political mobilisation promoting some form of collective self-interest. Not for one second do I pretend to know the 'whole' or 'real' story of what happened in the old South Africa, or what is happening in the 'new'. I know that significant parts of what has been, or is being invented, are not the way I experienced it.

For example, in early 2000, I was sitting next to General George Meiring at a discussion workshop in a hotel near Hermanus. He was the last head of the SADF under President de Klerk and the first under President Mandela. The theme of the workshop, which was attended by young Israeli and Palestinian intellectuals, students and journalists, was to find out if some of the 'magic' of our transition could rub off on their situation. Heribert Adam, a close friend and former academic colleague from Simon Fraser University in Vancouver, had made it depressingly clear that there was very little joy to be had for Israel and Palestine from our transition. (He and his wife, Prof. Kogila Moodley, have subsequently written a book about this, so

I will not repeat their compelling arguments: H Adam and K Moodley, *Seeking Mandela*.)

And then, FW de Klerk came on: 'First,' he said, 'I made sure that I had my party, my people and the state behind me. Then I made sure I had the majority of Whites behind me. And then I could release Mandela and face the risk of the negotiations', or words to that effect. I glanced sideways and saw Meiring shaking his head with a look of incredulity on his face. 'So, General, what do you say?' I asked. In Afrikaans he said, 'Hel, hy vat 'n bietjie kortpad met die waarheid.' Literally translated: 'Hell, he takes a bit of a short cut with the truth.'

Over drinks that evening, he elaborated by saying that when De Klerk made his famous 2 February 1990 speech, it came as a complete surprise to most in the security establishment. They knew that a policy shift had to come, in fact most of the top generals, including Meiring and particularly Constand Viljoen, made it clear repeatedly that there was no military solution to South Africa's problems and that a political one had to be found. De Klerk called the generals together in November and told them that he was mindful of their views and was thinking along those lines, particularly to avoid the folly of having Mandela die in prison. But the scope of De Klerk's reforms, and the complete lack of consultation to prepare for the consequences, caught the security establishment off guard. Meiring said that once the speech became public, he, as head of the defence force, was concerned that there would be some kind of internal revolt.

In the few months prior to the onset of negotiations, I had some discussions with General Constand Viljoen and he made no secret that, on behalf of the military, he felt a deep sense of betrayal and anger. He and other generals were urged from various quarters to stage a coup. (Read *Days of the Generals* by Hilton Hamann, for a fascinating account of this period.) 'I have 30 000 men under arms who will rise at a moment's notice,' he told me a number of times in those first few months. Viljoen, who is an expert on revolutionary warfare, was well aware of the folly of a coup option, but he was also very frustrated and angry at the political marginalisation of, what he saw as, the interests of the Afrikaner minority through the unfolding process of negotiations. And for this, he put the blame squarely on De Klerk's shoulders.

I was so concerned about Viljoen's anger and his intended abandonment of the whole process of negotiations that I managed to raise some foreign funds (West Germany) to employ his identical twin brother Braam to help with involving Constand in the process. Braam used to be professor of Theology at UNISA, and later worked for IDASA. Through Braam and Jurgen Kögl's efforts, Constand Viljoen met Mandela, Mbeki, Zuma and others at Jurgen's home. (Jurgen is a friend and former business colleague, and he did invaluable work in trying to contain a right-wing revolt.)

'Ja, man,' Meiring said to me, 'I know all about Constand and his 30 000, but it would not have worked and Constand knew it. We talked about the coup option and Constand said to me: "You know, George, if you and I wanted to, we can take over this country tomorrow." "Yes," I said, "it is true. But you and I also know that if we did, what do we do the next day?"'

I pointed out to General Meiring that one of the most extraordinary aspects of our transition was the complete collapse of the National Security Management System (NSMS). One of the first acts of FW de Klerk when he became president was to dismantle the NSMS as well as downgrade the significance of the National Security Council (NSC).

'Yes, it is true,' conceded Meiring, 'we were very powerful those days, but you must remember, the military never had any separate political ambition. We followed the British tradition, we were loyal to and served the government of the day.'

For me, this comment was so loaded with unintended irony and contradiction that it was hard to keep a straight face. 'The Government of the Day' in this instance was a racially entrenched White minority government that subjected the vast majority of South Africans to second-class citizenship, and such a situation could never have been maintained without the active and sustained support of the military, the police and their various extensions, i.e. 32nd Battalion, Koevoet, CCB, etc. The military may not have had any independent political ambitions, but they were politically deeply implicated. With a system of compulsory military conscription they indoctrinated thousands of young White South Africans on their patriotic duty to combat the 'total onslaught' of international communism and the ANC by being part of the 'total strategy' to preserve the status quo. If the military kept their side of the bargain by having no separate political ambition, why did those who governed not keep their side of the bargain by accepting political responsibility for what those in

18

security had to do under their policy directives? This is one of the paradoxes that remained unanswered at the conclusion of the TRC process. The politicians got off scot-free, whereas those in security felt they were subjected to a witch-hunt. (Read in particular Eugene de Kock's account of this in the book edited by J Gordin: *A Long Night's Damage*. He vividly portrays the nature of politicians' involvement in the dirty work of, particularly, Koevoet, which he helped to create. De Kock is presently serving a 212-year sentence for multiple murder committed by him personally, but is adamant that cabinet ministers who served on the National Security Council were aware of his work. In fact, two of them gave him medals for distinguished service. De Kock repeatedly makes the point that not only the top officers, but cabinet ministers, foreign affairs, police, defence, etc. were not only aware of but approved the 'war against terror'.)

To this day, General Meiring is still convinced that he was simply an impartial, loyal civil servant. I remember vividly the day Mandela was inaugurated as the first democratically elected president of South Africa in 1994. General George Meiring, head of the SADF, awaited his arrival at the Union Buildings for the oath-taking ceremony. I was standing at the top level looking down. The official car drove up, Mandela got out, and George Meiring clicked his heels, stiffened his back and saluted him. I had gooseflesh at the symbolic profundity of that moment.

This view of the impartiality of the security establishment and in particular the SADF was personally re-affirmed to me a few months after the conference that

General Meiring and I attended. I had lunch with Colonel Jan Breytenbach, brother of Breyten, retired soldier and a key figure in the famous 32nd Battalion. (His books on his involvement in the military include *Forged in Battle*, *They Lived by the Sword* and *The Buffalo Soldiers*.) The main purpose of 32nd Battalion was to be a highly professional reconnaissance and fighting unit to combat SWAPO, the Cubans, Russians and Fapla in Angola; and Frelimo in Mozambique; and to support Savimbi and UNITA and FNLA in Angola. Breytenbach became something of a military legend in his active career (read Piet Nortjé: *32nd Battalion*, and De Wet Potgieter: *Contraband: SA and the International Trade in Ivory and Rhino Horn*). He was a soldier's soldier, and fearless in battle. Those who served under him, Black and White, speak with obvious reverence about his qualities. Breyten Breytenbach and I were at a filling station somewhere en route to Grahamstown, when the attendant (a Black man) looked intently at Breyten and asked: 'Do you know Jan Breytenbach?' (Breyten and Jan do look alike.) Breyten replied, 'Yes, he is my brother, but we don't talk to each other.' The attendant said: 'I fought with him. That man is a soldier.' (Breyten and Jan have since reconciled. In fact, during the lunch Jan Breytenbach said to me: 'Tell my brother to stop kicking his dung around like some cantankerous old rhino, and tell him to come home.') Colonel Jan Breytenbach was also a very keen conservationist, and has documented his revulsion for senior politicians (i.e. cabinet ministers) and some senior officers of the SADF who enthusiastically participated in destroying virtually the total elephant and rhino population in Angola. (Read

Breytenbach: *The Plunderers*, as well as De Wet Potgieter mentioned earlier.)

'Ja,' said Breytenbach, 'George Meiring is right. We never really cared about politics. But those politicians from PW Botha onwards were useless. They could never make up their mind, or really knew what we were doing on the front. They often kept us in the dark, and we also did the same to them. One thing, however, was certain, I and those of us fighting there never believed a military solution to our problems was possible and we repeatedly told the politicians.' (This does not mean that he was unaware that by killing SWAPO's 'terrorists' and communists he was playing an indirect political role.)

I suggested to him that the withdrawal of military involvement by the Americans in 1975 must have been of decisive significance. He agreed, although militarily he did not think it would have been such a problem. The problem was that 'South Africa would be holding the political baby on its own'. At that time the idea was that a government of national unity would be established in Angola by 11 November 1975, but only if Angola was 'militarily secure'. The SADF was confident of achieving this, but only if the Americans were in the frame. I have not met one senior SADF officer of that period who was not convinced that the SADF could cope with the military side of the conflict, including the 'famous battle of Cuito Cuanavale'. They repeatedly stressed that it was a political, not a military problem.

A CIA official, John Stockwell, wrote about his experiences in Angola at this time in a book entitled *In Search of Enemies*, and his first chapter was called 'Kissinger's

21

Grunt'. Apparently the security and intelligence agencies were discussing the Angola situation in Washington, and Kissinger, as secretary of state, was asked whether the USA should continue supporting South Africa in its Angola initiative. Kissinger apparently grunted non-committally and left the meeting. Those who stayed spent hours trying to decide whether the grunt meant 'yes' or 'no', and concluded it was in the negative. (This negative 'grunt' was formally ratified in the US Congress in early 1976 by the so-called Dick Clarke Amendment.)

One of my first duties as defence spokesman for the Progressive Party in parliament was to visit the so-called 'operational area' with an all-party group of parliamentarians. This was precisely at the time of the 'Kissinger grunt' in 1975. None of us, including members of the ruling National Party, had the faintest idea of the extent of South Africa's involvement in South West Africa (Namibia), Angola, Rhodesia or Mozambique, which was, in any case, repeatedly denied by John Vorster (a keen hunter), then prime minister. I remember before we left for the operational area, reading a piece in *Time* magazine showing South African troops about a hundred and twenty kilometres from Luanda, capital of Angola. I simply could not believe that this could be so.

In the study of the commissioner-general of Ovamboland, Jannie de Wet, General Magnus Malan (then head of the SADF) told General Constand Viljoen (then head of the army) to explain South Africa's military involvement. Viljoen pinned a little square map on the wall (the same as the one in *Time* magazine) and told us that South African troops were about a hundred and twenty kilometers away

22

from Luanda, and the idea was to secure Angola militarily so that a government of national unity could be formed and it was imperative that Savimbi, as head of UNITA, should be part of it. We all just sat there, speechless and stunned. Some of the Nationalist MPs were slightly grey in the face. How were they going to explain this to their constituents? (So this is where the conscripted kids were!)

I was sitting opposite General Magnus Malan in the back of a Land Rover after the briefing. He asked me, 'So what do you think?' I said: 'Dis 'n kolossale kakspul' ('a colossally shit situation'). He replied, 'Don't worry, we can get everybody out in 24 hours if we have to.' On the flight back to South Africa, General Constand Viljoen told us that the briefing was classified information and could not be used for public purposes. I told him that I would not agree to this under any circumstances, and fully intended raising this issue in parliament; which I subsequently did, and which so infuriated PW Botha, then minister of defence, that he shouted to me across the floor that I would never be invited to the operational area again. I certainly did not cry myself to sleep over that. (In any case, I did go again, as a member of the parliamentary cricket team.) At that time, my half-brother, Sean Taylor, was doing his military service and was in control of a Panhard armoured car. I asked Viljoen where he could possibly be. Viljoen replied that he must be deep in Angola. I expressed shock, and said to Viljoen that a Panhard was no match for a Russian T34 tank. He said, 'As long as it does not rain, he will be OK.'

However, after Viljoen's presentation, we had a dinner reception at Jannie de Wet's house. PW Botha was also present. He was slightly tipsy, and through intelligence sources had obviously been informed of the consequences of 'Kissinger's grunt'. He grabbed hold of my arm and said, 'If it was not for the fucking Americans, we could take Luanda and Windhoek tomorrow. In fact we could take the whole of Africa.' That was the first time I realised the extent to which he was an extremely limited and dangerous individual. (Also, a keen hunter.)

Today (2005) some of the young men who fought in 32nd Battalion, Koevoet (a police interrogation unit) and other units of the security setup, are scattered around the world working for international security agencies. Early in 2005 I spent a night at Thula-Thula Game Lodge in Empangeni. The owner, Lawrence Anthony, single-handedly decided to save the Baghdad Zoo. He did, too, and received quite a lot of international publicity. I asked him how long he had stayed in Baghdad. He said about six months. I asked, 'How on earth did you survive the security situation?' He replied, 'If it was not for about two hundred Afrikaner recces, I could not have survived. These were real young killers and they worked closely with the American forces taking out suspicious locals.' Then he added, 'But give them a braai with a few beers and let Dozi sing "Ou Ryperd" and they cry like babies.' A cameraman for Fox TV who regularly visited Baghdad told me (May 2005) that there were about four-and-a-half thousand South Africans working there. Breyten Breytenbach, brother of Jan, came across two recces on Goree Island off the coast of Dakar. They were smuggling every movable thing up and down the West Coast of Africa; drugs, arms, diamonds, gold, etc. Breyten asked them, 'Why don't you go back to South Africa?' They replied, 'What for? There is nothing for us there, and here we make between ten and fifteen thousand US dollars a month. At least we can look after our families back home.' Chris Louw in his book *Boetman is die Bliksem In* writes poignantly about how some recces suffering from post-traumatic stress syndrome met regularly for a braai in the bush near Brits, got drunk, cried and reminisced about the 'old days'. These recces were soldier's soldiers, but were thoroughly led up the garden path and betrayed by their political masters.

So, when General George Meiring said to me at the workshop, after listening to De Klerk's bit of self-serving invention, that it was the first he had heard of this, I believed him. The simple and obvious question is: How could De Klerk know that 'I had everybody behind me' before he made his 2 February 1990 speech? He was never part of the inner circle of the cabinet, the NSMS or the NSC when PW Botha was prime minister. In fact, PW Botha disliked him and did not trust him (read Hamann mentioned earlier). As state president, FW de Klerk almost immediately abolished the NSMS and downgraded the NSC. He did not trust most of the top generals or officers, and on 20 December 1992 fired 23 of them. This was after the Goldstone Commission Report into 'third Force' activities. In fact, by the time he made his 2 February speech there was no overall security body he could consult, and he did not trust most of the top hierarchy in any case. Did he consult the Broederbond, his cabinet or his caucus? Not if I have to believe some of the members of each with whom I had extended conversations. In fact, De Klerk is on record as saying that not even his wife knew what he was going to say as they were driven to parliament for him to deliver the speech.

And yet, I do not believe De Klerk was completely dishonest when he made that speech at the workshop. That he was inventing some self-serving history is not in doubt. But by 1989 it was widely accepted, domestically as well as internationally, that apartheid or separate development and its derivatives, i.e. the Tricameral Parliament and homeland governments, was not going to work. The whole edifice was coming apart at the seams. Chester Crocker, then assistant secretary of state for Africa in the United States administration, provides a vivid account of how the security and political situation had fundamentally shifted in the sub-region, i.e. Namibia, Angola, Zimbabwe and Mozambique (read *High Noon in Southern Africa*). In a sense, De Klerk could claim that there was widespread support of the view that continuation with the existing policy in South Africa was untenable. But consensus on the untenability of the present in no way can be confused with what had to be done to change the course of things. In fact, had De Klerk circulated his speech beforehand to the generals, the cabinet, his parliamentary caucus and the Broederbond governing body, he would have been shot down in flames. His intervention was extremely fortuitous, individual and extraordinarily audacious, and history surely owes him a debt of gratitude for what he did. He co-opted and compromised every significant interest group and support base with the commitments made in his speech.

It was precisely the experience of being co-opted by De Klerk's commitment, e.g. releasing Mandela unconditionally, unbanning the ANC and other organisations, scrapping cornerstones of apartheid and security laws, and going for open-ended negotiations, that created a sense of betrayal amongst some in the security establishment, the Broederbond, cabinet, caucus and party. At the same time, there was very little, if anything, short of violent disruption that any of them could do to stop the process that was becoming increasingly irreversible. Even the ANC was co-opted into the process.

I am still amazed by how De Klerk somehow persists with claiming that what he did was simply the seamless unfolding of accepted Nationalist Party policy. I had an hour's in-depth discussion with him on a TV chat show on the KykNet Channel (2004). I asked him: 'When did you, and/or the NP, accept the principle of majority rule?' 'Oh,' he said, 'this was accepted as party policy at the NP Congress in February 1986.' Immediately after the show I took three phone calls, one from Pik Botha, former minister of foreign affairs, one from Barend du Plessis, former minister of finance, and one from Roelf Meyer, chief negotiator and former minister of constitutional development. They were all three very agitated, and independently claimed that 'FW was lying through his teeth'. I said to them that they could solve the problem of what to do on the next week's chat show by appearing on a panel, which they did. They tore FW apart in terms of his involvement of party, caucus and cabinet in making his speech. They also referred to the extraordinary difficulty they, especially Roelf, had in contacting FW de Klerk during critical moments of the negotiating process. (It was at the time when De Klerk's marriage was packing up and he was

having an affair with his current wife. It could not have
been an easy time for him.)

The other extraordinary thing was that I gained the
impression, from De Klerk, that he felt he could control
the process he had unleashed. We had a personal discussion in his office in Tuynhuis, a few weeks after he made
the speech, and I asked him, 'Why did you do it?' He
replied, 'Two reasons: I underwent a spiritual leap (geeste-
like sprong), in which I accepted the moral untenability
of apartheid, and secondly, I would have been a fool not
to take the gap that the fall of the Berlin Wall and the collapse of communism gave me.' He was convinced that he
had the ANC at a serious disadvantage.

This was subsequently borne out in a conversation I
had with Tjol Lategan (not the rugby player), a friend of
De Klerk's, who at the time (1991) served with me on the
Metropolitan Chamber (a bargaining structure that was
the result of a compromise between Olaus van Zyl, then
administrator of the Transvaal, and Cyril Ramaphosa, who
represented Soweto). Tjol also came from Pietersburg
(now Polokwane), where I grew up, and in the 'new
South Africa' he was a lonely member for the Nationalist
Party on the provincial council of the Northern Province.
I asked him at lunch one day, 'Tjol, what does FW think
he is going to achieve?' He said, 'Don't you worry, Van
Zyl. We are not capitulating. FW will pull them into
negotiations and then mark time for ten years.' I told him,
'You do not know with whom you are dealing.' Nothing
captures this folly better than General George Meiring's
own words: 'After the inauguration I was asked to sit at
the table of the president. I don't know why I was selected.

FW de Klerk also sat at the main table – he said to me while watching the fly-past and other proceedings, "We really needn't have given in so easily" (his words). I said to him, "But you never used your strong base to negotiate from, you never used the military as a base of strength, which you had available to you, you never wanted to use it." He just stopped speaking, and we didn't speak after that any more. There haven't been good vibes between us since that day' (Hamann above, p. 227).

There was a prevailing view in governing circles, largely fed by the intelligence community, that the ANC was in disarray toward the end of the 80s; that there were disputes about leadership and strategy, unresolved issues between the exile and domestic arms of the movement, as well as serious ideological fault lines. It was well known that agents of the apartheid state had infiltrated the ANC, both domestically and abroad, and that a network of 'impimpis' (informers) was quite active. (Again, read De Kock for an illuminating insight on how he 'turned' ANC activists into state security operatives – Askaris, as they were called by the security establishment, and 'impimpis' by the ANC.) Toward the end of PW Botha's era contacts were made between members of the governing establishment, e.g. PW Botha, Kobie Coetzee, Niël Barnard (National Intelligence Service – NIS), Prof. Willie Esterhuyse, and Mandela and ANC exiles such as Mbeki. Even Piet de Lange, then chairman of the Broederbond, met Thabo Mbeki in New York. There was a general feeling that these were 'nice guys one could talk to'.

The perception that the ANC was in some disarray during the '80s was not completely without foundation.

Soon after I left parliament in February 1986, and after the formation of IDASA (Institute for a Democratic Alternative for South Africa) by Alex Boraine and myself, a number of meetings were arranged by IDASA and the ANC in exile, and various people from inside. The meeting that is mentioned to the exclusion of almost all others was the one that took place in Dakar in July 1987. In fact, there were at least six other meetings. One of them was at Leverkusen, West Germany, where some of us from inside were going to meet with communists within the ANC and 'real live' communists from Moscow. That is how I met Slava Tetioken, then secretary-general of the Afro-Asian Solidarity Committee. It was based in Moscow and was chiefly responsible for funneling arms, funds and other forms of support to the ANC. Also present was Ambassador Solodovnikov and Vladimir Shubin. The latter I met again in Moscow in December 1988, and since then he has written a voluminous account of the Soviet Union's support for the ANC in his book *The ANC: A View from Moscow*. Slava and I became good friends, and he remains an unreconstructed old-fashioned Stalinist. We constantly bait each other, and after the bombing of the Twin Towers he brought Anatoly Karpov, the chess master, to my house for dinner. I asked Slava, 'Who bombed the Twin Towers?' He replied, 'Bush, of course, who else? He needed a pretext to expand international capitalism to the Middle East.' 'But,' I said, 'What about Osama Bin Laden?' 'Oh,' said Slava, 'very simple. He is a CIA agent.' (He really believes this stuff.)

Oom Bey Naudé and I were seated next to each other on the flight to Frankfurt for the Leverkusen meeting. If anyone had reliable knowledge of the inner workings of the ANC, it was Oom Bey. I turned to him during the flight and asked, 'What do you think would happen to the ANC if the NP government released Mandela, unbanned everybody and offered to start open–ended negotiations?' He laughed, 'They would be caught completely off guard. They are nowhere near ready for such an event.' At those IDASA meetings between 1987 and 1989 there was a fierce debate within the ANC between those in favour of negotiations (Mbeki and his supporters) and those dead against (Slovo, the communists and the militants).

When I was Tanner Lecturer at Brasenose, Oxford, in 1988, I gave my views at a workshop why I thought that a negotiated solution was the only viable option for resolving the South African dilemma. (I had already spelled out this position in detail in early 1985, before I met the ANC in Lusaka. Read GF Jacobs: *South Africa, The Road Ahead*, Chapter II 'Alternative Political Models'.) There were a few young ANC exiles present. Afterwards, one of them came up to me and said, 'One of the advantages of being in exile is that you know exactly what the ANC leadership is thinking. You, from the inside, would never know, especially if you are not part of the ANC. There is not the slightest chance of negotiations taking place. It will either be a successful revolution or the struggle continues.'

The last meeting IDASA arranged between people inside and the ANC in exile was in Marly le Roy in Paris, September 1989. At that time I was Visiting Fellow at All Souls, Oxford, and had lunches, drinks and discussions with Thabo Mbeki and Aziz Pahad in London before the

Paris meeting. The theme of that meeting was 'A Future Economic Policy for South Africa'. A passionate White trade-unionist got to his feet, pointing a quivering finger at some of the businessmen present – Ken Owen, former editor of the *Sunday Times*, was also there. 'You fat cats have had your chance,' the trade-unionist thundered. 'When we take over there will be no private property, industry will be fully nationalised, and the state will be the only real instrument for economic development.' In other words, standard Marxist-Leninist waffle: a national democratic revolution will sweep away the capitalist system and replace it with democratic centralism and a planned economy. I remember Ken Owen coming out of the meeting almost in shock: 'God save us if this lot take over.' The trade-unionist was Alec Erwin who subsequently became Minister of Trade and Industry and is now (May 2005) Minister of Public Enterprise, and defends free trade and a market economy with equal passion. A strong faction within the ANC, before the onset of negotiations, believed there was 'no middle road' (the title of Joe Slovo's paper after the 1985 ANC Kabwe Conference), and were committed to a successful revolutionary overthrow of the South African regime.

But even after De Klerk's speech in February 1990, and when preparations for negotiations were at an advanced stage, there was confusion and ambiguity within ANC ranks. Vula, an underground intelligence network, was created in 1980 in exile, and its purpose was to prepare the domestic situation for a violent/revolutionary change. During early July 1990, and as a direct result of information at its disposal, the security branch of the South

African police conducted certain follow-up, search-and-seizure operations in the Durban area. These investigations were to reveal the existence of a SACP/ANC plot aimed at utilising the space and freedom of movement created by the negotiation process in order to bring about a revolutionary and violent overthrow of the government of the time (my reference is an unpublished manuscript by Lieutenant Colonel James Brough Taylor, who at the time of his retirement on 31 March 1994 was in Crime and Intelligence Headquarters in Pretoria).

The point to remember is that those who planned Operation Vula were not a bunch of ANC romantics or some young hotheads. It is true that Mandela and Mbeki knew nothing about it, but externally it had the blessing of OR Tambo and Joe Slovo, Jacob Zuma, and by then internally of Mac Maharaj, Ronnie Kasrils and Siphiwe Nyanda. All of them had a deep mistrust of the viability of negotiations. I quote Siphiwe Nyanda, alias 'Gebuza', alias 'Carl', writing under the pseudonym Tebogo Kgope in *The African Communist*, no. 12, First Quarter 1990:

'Passivity does not contribute towards seizure of power. Negotiations for power are not part of an agenda to increase the militancy of the masses. Negotiations can only be conducted from a position of strength derived from militant action and other revolutionary activity by the oppressed.' (He was, of course, until recently head of the SANDF.) So, while Mandela and Cyril Ramaphosa were exploring the path of negotiation, Tambo and others blessed an attempt at violent insurrection. Operation Vula's exposure infuriated Mbeki and Mandela, and led to the suspension of the armed struggle in December 1990.

But then the Berlin Wall had come down on 9 November 1989. It symbolised the fall of institutionalised communism. Early in 1989 I was in Moscow and already the signs of collapse were in evidence. Slava Tetioken talked with passionate hatred of Gorbachev's '*glasnost*' and '*perestroika*', and although he, Solodovnikov and Shubin were still largely supportive of the ANC, among others around them, there was a marked decline of enthusiasm, especially for MK and so-called armed liberation. Some spoke contemptuously of MK being a glorified fundraising exercise, a point repeated by Mwezi Twala and Ed Benard in their book *Mbokodo – Inside MK*. Twala was himself an incarcerated MK member at Quatro, the ANC detention camp in Angola. In fact, military documents from the SADF state that during the decade of the 1980s, only 4% of any kind of military engagements involved MK, and then only in hit-and-run and counter-insurgency actions. 'We never had one serious military engagement with MK,' General George Meiring said. By far the most serious military engagements were with the Cubans, Russians and Fapla in Angola, SWAPO in SWA ('Those SWAPOs could fight,' Colonel Jan Breytenbach said to me), and supporting Smith in Rhodesia and Renamo against Frelimo. The point is that there was not the slightest prospect of a successful war of liberation being waged by the armed movement of the ANC against the SADF. Nobody knew this better than Thabo Mbeki. 'We can't fight a bush war in South Africa,' he said to the *New York Times* on 20 June 1980. 'Look at the map. It is all developed. There are roads, radios and landing strips everywhere … Our masses have to serve as our bush. The Black community is our bush' (Hamann above, p. 123).

How those who planned Operation Vula could still believe 'the masses' could be 'mobilised' for a 'people's war' and 'popular uprising' is tucked away in the self-fulfilling assumptions of left-wing revolutionary theory.

It is a sweet irony that Mbeki, who in exile pushed for negotiations and was vilified by the 'Vula types', now, during his presidency, loves to use martial language to refer to the transition in South Africa: the 'combatants', who 'defeated White minority rule', the ANC 'fighting force' that 'led us to our liberation' (read *Africa: Define Yourself*, a collection of Mbeki's speeches, interviews and answers to questions in parliament, edited by Essop Pahad and Willie Esterhuyse). Even at the most recent ANC general congress (June 2005), the discussion document on organisational design of the ANC refers to the 'forceful overthrow of the apartheid regime' that 'toppled apartheid rule'. This is serious invention of ANC and South African history.

The fall of the Berlin Wall drove home some hard and unpalatable lessons to the ANC, and by the way, to the NP government. It certainly caught the ANC with their ideological pants round their knees. Suddenly a liberal democratic paradigm in politics, and a market-driven paradigm in the economy, became dominant. Again, nobody understood this, and the consequences it was going to have for the ANC as a liberation movement, better in the ANC than Thabo Mbeki. (This is a major theme of William Gumede's book *Thabo Mbeki and the Battle for the Soul of the ANC*.) Three months after the Wall came down, De Klerk made his 2 February 1990 speech. I was still at Oxford, and a few days later had lunch with Mbeki, Aziz Pahad and Dladla in London. They knew that they faced

THE OTHER SIDE OF HISTORY

an entirely new situation, and that there was no road map to follow (precisely what Oom Bey Naudé predicted on our flight to Leverkusen). That is why De Klerk could say to me, 'I would have been a fool not to take the gap that the fall of the Wall gave to me.'

But the significance of two other major ideological shifts were not immediately appreciated by either De Klerk or the ANC in exile. The fall of the Wall also meant that 'the West', in whatever form, was no longer available to help the apartheid government to fight against communism – there no longer was any organised communism. Secondly, and consequently, support for the ANC to combat racism and oppression became universalised, and – especially – the USA embraced it. Suddenly the ANC had a whole new range of allies. Not in their wildest dreams did they think the 'Capitalist West' would support them as 'a National Democratic Movement' to get rid of apartheid. Someone who sensed this almost immediately was Nelson Mandela. The first country he visited after his release was not Russia or some Scandinavian one, but the USA for a ticker-tape parade in New York. The Americans went bananas over him, and from that moment De Klerk was on the back foot. The issue was no longer how to save some semblance of constitutionally guaranteed gimmicks to preserve White minority participation in a future South Africa, e.g. minority veto, power sharing, rotating presidency, etc. These were some of the constitutional gimmicks De Klerk contemplated 'to mark time for ten years'.

Even when he lost the Potchefstroom constituency to the right-wing Conservative Party of Andries Treurnicht in 1992, and called an all-White referendum seeking a mandate to continue with negotiations, De Klerk tried to console Whites by saying that negotiations would not be an open-ended affair, with placards announcing: 'Negotiations Yes; Majority Rule – Never!' And yet, it became increasingly clear that once the politics had moved from repressive stability under the securocrats with the NSMS, to the politics of negotiations for a new constitution, the only issue was how to transfer White minority control to a new fully democratic constitution. The statement that De Klerk negotiated because he had 'his party, the state and the majority of Whites behind him' before he entered into those negotiations, is a joke. But equally, to accept that the ANC from 1912 to 1990 was committed to the creation of a liberal democratic constitution for South Africa, stretches credulity beyond endurance.

Despite this, both sides claim 'victory' when they invent history for the 'new South Africa'. There was no 'victory' in the sense of the vanquished and the victorious. What eventually emerged was a settlement, a compromise that was far removed from the outcome that either side had pursued for decades, or promised their supporters. However, there is no doubt that the ANC were the prime beneficiaries of a negotiated settlement, and De Klerk and his followers the losers. But to claim that the 'brave freedom fighters', 'MK heroes' and 'the revolutionary masses' 'crushed the racist imperialist rulers' blah-blah-blah etc. is so much stuff and nonsense. Callinicos in her hagiography of OR Tambo *Beyond the Yengeni Mountains* creates the impression that he was almost completely in charge of every unfolding event and steering the local situation resolutely towards negotiations. She blithely states that the final straw that broke the camel's back was 'the decisive defeat' of South African forces at Cuito Cuanavale in 1987 in Angola. This theme was uncritically propagandised by Pallo Jordan when in March 2005 he delivered a paper, *The Relevance of Pan Africanism Today*, in which he says: 'Among the pressures that finally compelled the apartheid regime to the negotiating table [as if the ANC always prioritised getting to the nego- tiating table – my insert] was the defeat suffered at Cuito Cuanavale'. This 'defeat' occurred at the height of PW Botha's control of the NP, and about three years before De Klerk made his speech that precipitated a process of negotiation. There was no decisive military outcome at Cuito Cuanavale; hostilities stopped because of a political stalemate. All parties – the Soviets, Cubans and South Africans – agreed to withdraw militarily, and that negotia- tions should determine the outcome. General Konstantin Shaganovitch was the Soviet general in overall charge, and generals Rafael Puro Diaz and Arnaldo Ochea Sanchez were in charge of Cuban involvement. The latter was a dazz- ling war hero, and highly rated by the South African com- mand. He was also tipped to be Castro's successor. Castro used the stalemate to launch a massive propaganda offensive about 'a decisive victory'. I had to listen for three hours to the Cuban ambassador in Lusaka boasting about 'the vic- tory of Cuito Cuanavale' without providing a shred of tan- gible evidence. If it was such a decisive victory, why did Castro have his war hero, General Arnaldo Ochea Sanchez, executed by firing squad soon after Cuito Cuanavale on trumped-up charges of treason and drug peddling? Some say that Castro was jealous of him receiving too much glory for the 'victory'. (I hold no brief for South Africa's military involvement in the sub-region. Many times Magnus Malan, as minister of defence, accused me of 'singing in Moscow's choir' for criticising our involvement. If only he knew how the ANC altar boys in 'Moscow's choir' were berating me as well, he would have calmed down.) It is not necessary to invent victories and defeats to understand how negotiations came about and the ANC came out of them as the prime beneficiaries. So what happened?

Many, and I am sure better, books have been written on this question, and I am not going to repeat all the arguments. For me it is quite clear that both De Klerk and the ANC faced the same set of circumstances, for which neither was responsible but which each thought they could exploit to their own advantage. De Klerk genuinely thought he had the ANC at a disadvantage because of the fall of the Wall, and the ANC were reluctant and ambiguous about negotiations but saw how rapidly international support was flowing in their direction. The one started negotiations and ended up the loser; the other reluctantly entered into negotiations and ended up the prime beneficiary. Why?

De Klerk did not really have a clue about the security situation that he had inherited because he had deliberately been kept out of the loop. Eugene de Kock makes the point that because De Klerk sat in on NSC meetings (and he provides minutes documenting this), he could have found out if he wanted to. (When I asked him at that discussion in Tuynhuis, 'Do you know about the security situation you have inherited?', he became quite irritated and I simply said, 'I am glad I am not in your shoes.') The one who understood this perfectly was Mandela, and he used it to brilliant advantage to strengthen the ANC's bargaining position. I remember sitting in the back of his car with him, asking, 'What would you do when you are president and you go to Voortrekkerhoogte [military headquarters] and you say to the top twenty generals, "You're fired!" and they say, "We're not."?' His eyes widened and he said, 'That would be a very dangerous situation.' In retrospect I realise he was simply humoring me. He knew exactly how important the security issue was, and he badgered De Klerk mercilessly about it. The issue of a 'third force' and military destabilisation was continuously brought to De Klerk's attention, and De Klerk simply did not know how to respond. Mandela milked every ounce of sympathy for the ANC being the victims of a dirty-tricks campaign, and if anyone was single-handedly responsible for De Klerk firing 23 generals and top military officials, it was Mandela (read Hamann, Chapter 10). The violence at Boiphatong in June 1992 provided fertile propaganda for this.

But apart from that, the ANC simply had politically more astute and able negotiators than the NP. Here, Cyril Ramaphosa was head and shoulders above everyone else. Everybody talked about the 'Roelf and Cyril Show', but it was quite clear who the senior partner was. After the collapse of CODESA 2 and the violence of Boiphatong, the prospects of continued negotiations were hanging by a thread. Those prospects were kept alive by Roelf Meyer and Cyril Ramaphosa. When negotiations resumed after De Klerk accepted the ANC's 'sunset clause', Meyer, at a critical meeting of the Negotiations Committee, accepted the principle of majority rule. When he reported this to De

Klerk, De Klerk said in shock, 'My God, Roelf, you have given away the country.' Cyril told me that the moment Roelf accepted this principle on behalf of the government negotiating team, he (Cyril) asked for a 15-minute adjournment 'so that we could withdraw to our own room and laugh our heads off'. From here on negotiations went one way for the ANC and the other way for the NP.

The most serious bit of ANC invented history is Tambo and Mbeki's supposed role in negotiated transition. In both Callinicos's biography of Tambo, and Essop Pahad and Willie Esterhuyse's editing of Thabo Mbeki's speeches in *Africa: Define Yourself*, the name Cyril Ramaphosa does not get a single mention. Negotiations are presented as an exile-driven process controlled by Mbeki, and when De Klerk made his speech all the concessions had already been negotiated between Mbeki and the 'regime' by September 1989 (read the 'Biographical sketch of Thabo Mbeki', pp. 295–316). From top NIS officials I learned that De Klerk's first attempt to explore the way forward was to send Mike Louw and Maritz Spaarwater to accompany Willie Esterhuyse to meet Mbeki in Geneva. Surely all of this is a bit fantastical! Does Ramaphosa not deserve even a slight honourable mention? Mbeki hardly ever attended CODESA meetings and, according to Gumede (*Thabo Mbeki: The Battle for the Soul of the ANC*), spent most of his time eliminating potential opponents and trying to capture control of the ANC.

That De Klerk's speech precipitated a process of profound significance for a democratic and peaceful South Africa is without question, and nobody can, or should, deny him the credit and honour for it. But equally, making that speech with the foreknowledge that most likely he would abandon the cabinet, parliament and the NP within two years after the first democratic elections in South Africa is simply not credible, and the only valid conclusion to be drawn is that things did not exactly work out the way he had anticipated. His withdrawal from politics started the long drawn-out political hara-kiri of the NP which concluded ten years after the first democratic elections, when a few remaining political carpetbaggers in the NP joined the ANC as the governing party. Eventually, in 2005, the once-mighty NP that governed South Africa from 1948-1990 with remorseless brutality disbanded, and joined the ANC as ordinary members. Nobody could have anticipated that on 2 February 1990.

But who is to say I am not simply inventing history myself? Why should my invented history be better than the invented history of the Nats or of the ANC? Isn't it so that the party that is in power determines what history is? The Nats for more than forty years forced their invented history into the minds of millions of South Africans. Why can't the ANC do the same? Who am I to question either? All I said at the outset is that I simply did not experience it the way the Nats or the ANC presented it. The essence of sound historiography is doubt, or as Karl Popper, the philosopher, would say, 'conjecture and refutation'. Something new can always crop up to question prevailing certainties. The essence of invented history is dogmatic confidence. That is why, especially, officially invented history always prepares its own deconstruction. The burden of the great lie eventually becomes too heavy to bear.

CHAPTER 2

FROM DAKAR
TO DEMOCRACY

In 1974 I went to Parliament, and Breyten Breytenbach went to prison. In my case it was more coincidental, in Breyten's more failed intention than coincidence. He wanted to start an underground White non-communist youth movement called Okhela, and was promptly shopped by the communists in the ANC. He was sentenced to nine years' imprisonment, of which he served seven.

I was assured I could not win the Rondebosch constituency; that is why I accepted the nomination. By keeping the United Party workers away from helping in Sea Point, Colin Eglin could scrape it, and be a partner to Helen Suzman who had been alone in Parliament for 13 years, and was tired.

Academic life had drifted into a period of stagnation for me. I became professor and head of the Department of Sociology at Wits in 1973. I was 33, and spent most of my time planning undergraduate courses and being an academic housekeeper. Electoral experience seemed like a good exercise in participant observation. I was totally unprepared for what was to follow during the next 12 years.

In 1979 I became leader of the official opposition in Parliament. By then I had experienced the full weight of conservative Afrikaner nationalist hatred and vilification, but also began to see cracks of self-doubt beginning to surface in the ranks of the NP. Every passing day saw the foundations of apartheid/separate development begin to crumble and erode. The Grand Design was beginning to disintegrate.

PW Botha became president when I became leader of the opposition; no connection. But I used my new status to seek an appointment with him to ask him if I could visit Breyten in prison. He agreed. (From 1979 to 1986 when I resigned, I asked every year to visit Nelson Mandela in prison. The reply was that he was entitled to one 'Red Cross' visit a year, and that belonged to Helen Suzman. Breyten was released two years ahead of full time, and he and his wife Yolande left for Paris).

The NP government then, from 1980 onwards, started to go into a tailspin. Botha and his closest colleagues knew some new initiatives were necessary. They had been repeatedly told by the security establishment that a military, i.e. repressive, option was not possible. Botha appointed a Constitutional Commission chaired by Chris Heunis to explore alternative constitutional possibilities. The result was nothing short of pathetic. South Africa created a Tricameral Constitution which would bring Coloureds and Indians and Whites into a common parliament, some government of national unity for homeland Blacks, and limited municipal authority for urban Blacks. If anything was going to polarise and isolate South Africa, it was this kind of constitutional fraud.

Botha called a referendum in 1983 to seek White approval. On behalf of the Progs (Progressive Federal Party),

I vehemently opposed the Nationalists and urged for a 'No' vote. The *Sunday Times*, most of the business establishment and even a number of Prog supporters and representatives thought it was a 'step in the right direction', and urged voters to go for the 'Yes' vote. Dr Andries Treurnicht and I went for a 'No' vote, obviously for vastly different reasons. The 'No' vote got thumped. It also precipitated a strategy to make the townships ungovernable.

Harry Pitman, then MP for Pietermaritzburg and a close friend and confidante, is dead now, but if he was alive he would testify that the result of the referendum convinced me that the time had come to leave parliamentary politics. I said this to the leadership – Suzman, Eglin, De Beer, etc – but they urged me to stay on for one more year. I stayed for another two-and-a-half years. I mention this because there is a common fiction presented as fact that Thabo Mbeki and the ANC in exile persuaded me to leave Parliament. I met them with the PFP executive in October 1985 for the first time. The Tricameral referendum was in 1983. In early 1985 I again told Colin Eglin, De Beer, Suzman and HF Oppenheimer that continued membership of the Tricameral Parliament was a waste of time. The country had become stalemated between the politics of repression and the politics of revolt. The opposition in Parliament were simply passive spectators of a game in which they could not participate.

The PFP executive's visit to Lusaka in October 1985 to meet the ANC leadership certainly reinforced this view. There we met Mbeki, Zuma, Maharaj, Barbara Masekela and others. The official position conveyed to us was that the 'armed struggle' was the only way forward. (Personally

I thought this was a bit of a joke, based on my discussions with the SADF and security forces.) Mbeki did make it clear to me personally that 'talking was better than killing' and negotiations could be explored.

I went back and stated repeatedly in public that no resolution to South Africa's crises without the ANC was possible. That visit did bring home to me very forcibly how out of touch Parliament was with what was happening in South Africa. The NSMS and Botha knew, but they were not telling anybody. If anything, they systematically lied to Parliament about the situation.

The final straw that broke the camel's back was the systematic and deliberate violation of the Nkomati Accord which was signed between the South African government and the government of Mozambique on 16 March 1984, at the border town of Komatipoort in South Africa. I was present at the signing, and even congratulated President Botha on the initiative, saying it was the first sign that the South African government was moving away from a policy of regional aggression. How wrong can one be on such matters!

A certain Renamo officer, Colonel Vass, had his diaries captured by the Frelimo government. In them it was apparent that before, during and after the signing of the Nkomati Accord South Africa was destabilising Mozambique. I saw a very brief report on this in the daily press, and asked General Constand Viljoen for an explanation. He said it was just 'communist propaganda'. I was far from convinced.

Eglin and I were asked by the Australian and New Zealand governments to be their guests in mid-1985, and again on the flight over I said to Colin Eglin that we simply could not continue like this. He agreed, but said we must articulate an alternative strategy. He said he would, and I said I would. Colin Eglin never came round to formulating one; perhaps because he saw no alternative. I did formulate one, which in retrospect seems a bit far-fetched and was rejected by the PFP caucus when I put it to them (see Appendix I). On my return I again, in a private bugged conversation with PW Botha, pleaded with him to release Mandela unconditionally. He smiled and said I did not understand, but the majority of Blacks supported him. That was when I finally knew I was wasting my time. All this happened before I met Thabo Mbeki in Lusaka in October 1985. In December 1985 I contacted President Samora Machel's office in Maputo and asked for an interview to discuss the Vass diaries. He agreed immediately. My father-in-law and I flew down in a chartered one-prop aircraft. First, we were briefed by Sergio Vierra, Minister of Intelligence. He presented me with a copy of the Vass diaries which I have to this day. There was not the slightest doubt that the South African government was destabilising Mozambique on almost a daily basis.

'What does Botha think he is doing? I cannot fight a war against him. But tell him, like Hitler's war ended in Berlin, his war will end in Pretoria.' It was a highly agitated Machel walking up and down and waving his arms. Those turned out to be prescient words.

I resigned from Parliament, as leader of the opposition and member of the PFP, on 11 February 1986. Thabo Mbeki must have raised some eyebrows among his own group with the effusiveness of his response. 'Never in the history of our country has a White establishment political leader confronted the iniquity of the system of White minority domination as Dr Slabbert has today. We salute his courage, his honesty and his loyalty to a common South African nationhood ... Today millions of our people, of all races, will acclaim Dr Slabbert as a new Voortrekker.' Almost twenty years later, RW Johnson told me in a sepulchral whisper that I had no idea how much my esteem suffered in liberal circles because of my resignation. Ken Owen, at the time, called me an 'Afrikaner glamour boy' who 'whored with the English vote'. Nobody had the slightest interest in engaging me on the reasons I offered for my resignation. The local (White) communists of the ANC were deeply suspicious, even hostile, convinced I was part of some Trojan Horse plot to dilute and confuse the 'struggle'.

When I left I had no strategies or political plans whatsoever. All I knew was that I needed to find a job because I had R2 500 left after twelve-and-a-half years in Parliament. My whole gratuity (R120 000) went to pay off the housing loan that I borrowed from E Oppenheimer and Sons. Alex Boraine resigned a week after me. He also had no idea what he was going to do. We got together, and thus IDASA was born. (In the mean time I was offered visiting professorships from UWC and UCT. I never received a regular income from IDASA.)

From the outset, Boraine and I were determined that IDASA should be non-aligned, not part of 'the struggle' or the 'system', but that it should try to promote dialogue between members of each, or among young people, predominantly Afrikaners, who were isolated and confused.

From these efforts was born the meeting in Dakar between leaders of the ANC in exile and predominantly
Afrikaans-speaking professionals from inside South Africa.

The actual germ of the idea for a Dakar conference
came from a meeting I had with Breyten Breytenbach on
the island of Goree off the coast of Dakar. He would use
his position on France Liberté, Danielle Mitterrand's
organisation, and her friendship with Abdou Diouf, president of Senegal, to arrange a meeting as far away from
South Africa as possible. It was in raising funds for this
meeting that I first met George Soros, and I have been
involved with his Open Society Initiative ever since.

Almost eighteen years later, RW Johnson in his book
South Africa: The First Man, the Last Nation refers to 'endless missions' to Dakar, Lusaka, etc., where businessmen,
academics and professionals went to 'ingratiate themselves
with the new leaders' and 'negotiate a position for themselves' in the future South Africa. This is precisely what
the NP government and Nasionale Pers newspapers said
at the time of the Dakar meeting, i.e. that we were 'crawling to the ANC' on 'Dakar safaris'. There was only one
meeting in Dakar arranged by IDASA.

The list of people who attended the Dakar Conference
is contained in Appendix III. I leave it to the reader's
imagination as to how many of them would have gone on
'endless missions' to Dakar to arse-creep with their future
leaders, and what they are engaged in now. The opening
statement of a week-long discussion was made by Mac
Maharaj who said: 'Before I went to Robben Island I
killed in anger. After Robben Island I could kill in cold
blood.' This more or less set the theme that dominated

most discussions: violence vs. peaceful change; revolution vs. negotiation. The central question those from inside had to contend with was: 'What avenues for peaceful change remain, and what are we doing to explore them?' The central question that the ANC delegation had to contend with was: 'What are the prospects for successful revolutionary change, and what kind of society would have to be reconstructed should it succeed?' At the end of the Dakar session a joint communiqué was issued – see Appendix II.

Dakar, as an event, consisted of three parts: the conference in Dakar, a visit to Burkina Faso, where we were the guests of President Thomas Sankarra, and a visit to Accra in Ghana, as the guests of President Jerry Rawlings. These visits were covered extensively by the international media, and more than enough material is available in the archives of the Mayibuye Library on Robben Island. There it can also be seen that the SACP 'deployed' Anthony Holiday, journalist/scholar, and Anthony Trew, loyal foot-soldier and member of the SACP, to track me and assess the significance of Dakar within the overall struggle context. While they reported that Dakar was 'a good thing' that could 'weaken the enemy' and my lectures at Oxford as Tanner Lecturer as 'intellectually competent', I was not to be trusted as I was 'an opportunist', a 'showman', 'intellectually dishonest' and 'had an inflated view' of myself.

After Dakar and until 2 February 1990, I visited Beijing, Moscow, Amsterdam, London, Washington, the OAU Headquarters in Addis Ababa, Berlin and Leverkusen. In all of them, I either met with ANC representatives or government and/or opposition representatives sympathetic to their cause. With the exception of Moscow, everyone accepted armed struggle and continued confrontations as inevitable. It was winter time in Moscow, and we were met at the airport by the African Solidarity Committee in the form of Slava Tetioken and Ambassador Solodovnikov. Also present was Simon Makana (now deceased), the ANC representative who enjoyed full ambassadorial status. In fact, I drove with him to our hotel in his official car with the ANC flag waving on the bonnet. It was the end of 1988, and *perestroika* and *glasnost* were well under way. It was the first time I began to notice that the ANC might come under pressure to change their strategies, if not explicitly then implicitly, from one of their staunchest allies.

Early in 1988 I received an invitation from All Souls College, Oxford, to be a Visiting Fellow for a year. This was for the 1989/1990 academic year, and although it was for a full year I could only be there for two semesters, October to March. During this time, IDASA arranged its last meeting with the ANC at Marly le Roy in Paris, in November 1989. Before, we had organised meetings in Berlin, Leverkusen, Harare, Lusaka and New York, and discussed a wide range of issues, e.g. a future legal system, a future education system, culture and diversity, a future economy, etc. Despite a great deal of common ground, the overriding strategic position from the ANC was that the armed struggle had to be the primary driving force to achieve all of this. I certainly never agreed with this, hence my vilification and rubbishing from the militants and the SACP.

Back in South Africa important things were happening. PW Botha suffered a second stroke in January 1989, just

51

before the opening of Parliament. From his hospital bed he told the NP caucus to elect a parliamentary leader (note, not a new president). Botha desperately tried to cling to power, but in August 1989 was told by FW de Klerk (who narrowly won the parliamentary caucus election against Barend du Plessis) and Pik Botha, minister of foreign affairs, that he had to go. In effect, De Klerk was Acting President when he called for the last Tricameral general election on 6 September 1989. He won a decisive victory against the right wing, and claimed that he had received a mandate from the White electorate to seek a new political dispensation for South Africa based on a common constitution, and that this had to be negotiated with 'the genuine leaders' of the majority. He also made it abundantly clear that he would never accept majority rule or negotiate himself out of power (see in this regard Robin Renwick: *Unconventional Diplomacy in Southern Africa*; he was the British ambassador during this period, and had numerous discussions with De Klerk, and from various accounts he had a significant impact on De Klerk's thinking). On 15 October 1989 De Klerk released eight high-profile political prisoners, including Walter Sisulu. This was regarded as 'a de facto unbanning of the ANC'. Govan Mbeki had already been released. In November 1989 De Klerk disbanded the NSMS; the Berlin Wall came down, and IDASA held its last meeting with the ANC in Paris. I was at All Souls at the time of the meeting.

But, unbeknown to most of us, apparently representatives of 'the regime' had been holding secret talks with the ANC in exile, particularly Thabo Mbeki, since 1986. The key figure here was Professor Willie Esterhuyse who reported to, first, BJ Vorster, and then to PW Botha. So successful were his discussions with Mbeki that he introduced top members of the NIS to Mbeki in Geneva in early 1989, and by September 1989 a delegation led by Fanie van der Merwe, at the time director general for constitutional affairs, reached agreement between Mbeki and 'the regime' that 'all political prisoners, including Nelson Mandela, would be released; political parties would be unbanned, exiles allowed to return … subsequent to which negotiations for a new South Africa would begin' (*Africa: Define Yourself*, p. 314): precisely the issues that De Klerk would announce in his 2 February 1990 speech.

Let us just take a deep breath here. By August 1989 PW Botha was persuaded to relinquish power; by 20 September 1989 De Klerk was sworn in as president; at the same time, in September 1989, Mbeki had reached an agreement with 'the regime' on fundamental issues that De Klerk would announce in his speech on 2 February 1990 which the NP caucus, the NP, the security establishment, and no significant ANC figure, including Mandela, knew anything about, but which Mbeki and 'the regime' shared with each other. The questions simply are: What 'regime', and 'who' in 'the regime', had agreed? In what capacity did Mbeki negotiate this, and with a mandate from whom? Are we to believe that when negotiations slowly began to take shape between Mandela and De Klerk, what followed was simply a drama playing itself out after rehearsals? That CODESA 1 and 2 were not really to be taken seriously because Mbeki had already settled the

key issues and was simply waiting for the whole panto-
mime to play itself out!

Esterhuyse and Pahad go on to say (p. 314): 'Until these
actually happened, there were many in the ANC and its
supporters in South Africa and internationally, who
thought it was impossible for the South African regime to
agree to all these things. They were therefore convinced
that Mbeki and his team had betrayed the struggle by
holding out the illusion of a negotiated settlement.' Who
was in Mbeki's team? Did it include people from inside
South Africa (Mbeki was in exile at the time), e.g.
Ramaphosa? Mandela? Winnie? Chikane?

But why is all this historical invention necessary? Very
few would doubt Thabo Mbeki's qualities as a negotiator,
or his ability to persuade or charm. I myself was victim of
this. IDASA and its meetings with the ANC in exile does
not even get a dishonourable mention in Esterhuyse and
Pahad's biographical sketch of Mbeki. I have no problem
with that. We never pretended to negotiate on behalf of
anybody. We simply wanted to assist in making dialogue
with the ANC legitimate. In the half-a-dozen meetings
we had with the ANC in exile I learned an enormous
amount about the political dynamics of South Africa. I
also learned first-hand that the ANC in exile did not have
a single dominant strategy, but also that negotiations with
'the regime' were definitely not the unambiguous preferred one when compared to armed struggle. Mbeki
deserves to be commended for keeping this option alive.
Mandela was released on 11 February 1990, nine days
after De Klerk's speech. From then until 26 September
1993, with the signing of the Record of Understanding

between Mandela and De Klerk, South Africa went through some heavy corrugations:

- 'Operation Vula' in June 1990;
- violent clashes between Inkatha and the ANC in urban townships and KwaZulu-Natal;
- accusations of 'third force' activities to destabilise negotiations, made by Mandela to De Klerk;
- the break-up of CODESA 1 and then CODESA 2 after the violence of Boiphatong in June 1992.

The heaviest turbulence went largely unnoticed: that was the anger and threat posed by right-wing Afrikaans groups. During March and April 1993 General Constand Viljoen was beginning to attend AWB meetings at which Eugene Terre Blanche shouted continuously: 'The AWB or the ANC'. During this period, until the elections in April 1994, Thabo Mbeki and Jacob Zuma played a critical role in engaging the right wing and farmers. They also helped to bring Buthelezi and Viljoen into some settlement. In October 1993 through the kind assistance of Ambassador Ueberschaer, the West German ambassador, I managed to raise funds to pull in Braam Viljoen, brother of Constand, to help with engaging the right wing, particularly farmers, and Constand. Jurgen Kögl and Braam Viljoen did extraordinary work in this regard, and through their intervention Buthelezi and Constand Viljoen were brought on board. It was a close shave because General George Meiring told the De Klerk cabinet that if General Constand Viljoen was not part of a political settlement the SADF would split from the rank of major down. De Klerk sent Niël

Barnard to be part of the Kogl–Braam Viljoen discussions. Eventually the ANC and the right and Buthelezi (1994) agreed on vital constitutional principles such as mother-tongue education, the right of minorities, and self-determinism and constitutional governance. On 23 April 1994 at the West Wing of the Union Buildings this was witnessed among others by Ambassador Princeton Lyman (USA), Ambassador Anthony Reeves (UK), Walter Sisulu, Jurgen Kögl, Braam Viljoen, Aziz Pahad, General Tiny Groenewald and Baron Klaus von der Ropp.

Seven months after the signing of the Record of Understanding, the first democratic elections were held on 27 April 1994, but before then, as a result of the signing, Buthelezi and Constand Viljoen walked away from negotiations. A month before the elections, in March, the AWB 'invaded' Bophuthatswana. (It is said that De Klerk ordered NIS to induce them into Bop, and asked Viljoen to come out of retirement and help prevent the right wing destabilising elections. Before then some bombs went off in Braamfontein.) Soon after the invasion and just before the elections, Buthelezi and Viljoen agreed to participate. Although a meeting took place between Mandela and Buthelezi in January 1991, it was inconclusive, and right through Mandela's presidency an uneasy truce prevailed.

There is no doubt that in the run-up to the signing of the Record of Understanding, an extraordinary relationship between Roelf Meyer and Cyril Ramaphosa helped to keep the hope of negotiations alive. There is also no doubt that Ramaphosa was the chief negotiator on behalf of the ANC. (The Interim Constitution which was finally

Lagos, Nigeria 1975. (*Left to right*) NN Ukaegbu of the Cabinet Office Enugu,
F van Zyl Slabbert, C Eglin, Mr Blankson of the Ministry of External Affairs.

Dakar, July 1987. Breyten Breytenbach, Thabo Mbeki and Van Zyl Slabbert.

Burkina Faso, 1987. 'Oom Bey' Beyers Naudé, Van Zyl Slabbert and Thabo Mbeki.

Leverskusen, The Berlin Meeting, 1988

Back Row: Unknown, Theo Hanf, Breyten Breytenbach, Wynand Malan, Deon Geldenhuys, Hermann Giliomee, André du Toit, Lawrence Schlemmer

4th Row: Thabo Mbeki, Gerhard Erasmus, Jackie Selebi, Beyers Naudé, S Booysens, Heribert Adam, T Seedat, Frances Kendall

3rd Row: Gerhard Rachile, Unknown, Simon Makana, Joe Slovo, Irena Filatova, Mark Swilling

2nd Row: Hennie Kotzé, Aziz Pahad, Sampie Terreblanche, Slava Tetioken, Anne-Marie Mischke, Van Zyl Slabbert, John Barrow, Willie Breytenbach

Front Row: Alex Boraine, Ambassador Solodovnikov, Johnny Makatini, Jenny Boraine

The Dakar
delegates, 1987.

1. Lourens du Plessis
2. Penuel Maduna
3. Johan van der Westhuizen
4. Jimi Matthews
5. Hennie Serfontein
6. Manie van Rensburg
7. Essop Pahad
8. Willem van Vuuren
9. Andrew Savage
10. Grethe Fox

11. Tommy Bedford
12. Wayne Mitchell
13. Gerhard Erasmus
14. Blackie Swart
15. Breyten Breytenbach
16. Leon Louw
17. Revel Fox
18. Ampie Coetzee
19. Jaap du Randt
20. Francis Meli

21. Peter Gastrow
22. Phillip Verster
23. Barbara Masekela
24. Thabo Mbeki
25. Beyers Naudé
26. President Sankara
27. Ilse Naudé
28. Van Zyl Slabbert
29. André P Brink
30. Alex Boraine

31. Heribert Adam
32. Christo Nel
33. Chris Louw
34. Jacques Kriel
35. Hardy Botha
36. Franklin Sonn
37. Randall van der Heever
38. Trudie de Ridder
39. Ian Liebenberg
40. André Odendaal

(Photo: Rashid Lombard)

Van Zyl Slabbert and Breyten Breytenbach (*right of Slabbert*), the masterminds behind the Dakar conference, leading the conversation. (Photo: Rashid Lombard)

Winds of change ... Dakar 1987. A young Thabo Mbeki and Hennie Serfontein in conversation with Jimi Matthews (*front row*), Breyten Breytenbach and Manie van Rensburg (*right, seated in the second row*) and, Allister Sparks, (*seated extreme right in the third row.*) (Photo: Rashid Lombard)

Dakar, 1987. Thabo Mbeki and Beyers Naudé near Ougadougou, helping to erect a monument against apartheid. (Photo: Rashid Lombard)

Moscow, 1989. Enos Mabuza, Jane Slabbert, Simon Makana (ANC Representative in Moscow), Van Zyl Slabbert, Ambassador Solodovnikov, Unknown lady, Prof Johan Degenaar from the University of Stellenbosch, Slava Tetioken, Vladimir Shubin (both from the Afro-Asian Solidarity Committee).

The plaque President Diouf unveiled in June 1992.

June 1992. Van Zyl Slabbert welcomes President Abdou Diouf of Senegal to Goree Island for the launch of the Goree Institute. Breyten Breytenbach to the right of Slabbert.

agreed upon bore an uncanny resemblance to PFP constitutional proposals. This leads me to the conclusion that Eglin must have been punching way above his weight, because neither the ANC nor the NP knew much about a liberal democratic constitution. Prof. Marinus Wiechers, professor of Constitutional Law at UNISA at the time, and Colin Eglin were both thoroughly familiar with the constitutional structure of a liberal democracy, and must have had a disproportionate influence on the final product. Even to this day, at the end of 2005, the ANC high command either disrespects or does not understand the fundamentals of a liberal democratic constitution. Eglin continued into the new democratic Parliament, and justifiably developed the status of an elder statesman.) Thabo Mbeki was seldom, if ever, in evidence. Maybe behind the scenes he played a crucial role, but how are we to know? The more one probes, the less one finds out. For example, a senior cabinet colleague of De Klerk's told me that he has no recollection of Esterhuyse negotiating on behalf of De Klerk with Mbeki, or Mbeki reaching an agreement with the De Klerk 'regime'.

I do not want to be understood as having a personal vendetta against Mbeki. I definitely do not. Whenever I reflect on our past friendship, it is with a sense of sadness. From October 1985 until he became deputy president in 1994, we met often and were comfortable in each other's company. Some of our meetings in exile were hectic with partying and carousing. Planning the Dakar Conference with him in London was extremely exciting. Once he returned from exile I helped him find a penthouse in Hillbrow; that is how I introduced him to Jurgen Kögl, whose penthouse it was. I also asked him to help resolve the Mercedes-Benz strike in East London, which together with Slovo and Steve Tshwete he did. I introduced him to Levett of Old Mutual, and some Anglo American Corporation heavies.

We met socially a number of times. Not once during this period did he talk about how negotiations were going, or his role in them. And then he became deputy president. Just before, I met him at Aziz Pahad's wedding and he said, 'Van Zyl, where have you been hiding?' I said, 'You are the busy one. I am simply a phone call away.' He said, 'Come and see me tomorrow night.'

He and Zanele had moved into an apartment in Killarney by then. It was a Sunday evening, and when I arrived I saw that there was a small queue of people waiting to see him. Eventually I was alone with him, and he seemed quite awkward and out of place. 'What would you do if you were to become deputy president?' he asked. I said, 'I would appoint a number of committees of experts in key areas to constantly remind me of how much I have to learn and how ignorant I am.' This must have offended him. Why? I have no idea. But it was the end of our comfortable relationship. He is the only person I know who demonstrated to me that my friendship was expendable.

What is often overlooked in that period, 1994–1999, i.e. the period of Mandela's presidency, is that South Africa was not governed under the current and final democratic constitution. Therefore, to celebrate ten years of democracy in 2004 is technically speaking not correct. From 1994 to 1999 South Africa was governed by a Government of National Unity (GNU) under an Interim Constitution.

In the GNU there were two deputy presidents, Mbeki and De Klerk, and a multi-party cabinet that was supposed to take decisions on the basis of consensus. I know that Cyril Ramaphosa, who was Mandela's preferred choice, was deeply disappointed that he did not get the deputy presidency and that it went to Thabo. (Gumede has written extensively about this and other activities in the run-up to Mbeki's presidency: *Thabo Mbeki and the Battle for the Soul of the ANC*.) Ramaphosa was appointed chairman of the Constituent Assembly which had to finalise the Constitution. Again he performed with extraordinary competence, and by 1996 the Constitution was certified by the Constitutional Court under the leadership of Arthur Chaskalson. The moment the final Constitution was certified De Klerk resigned his deputy presidency and all other political positions. He experienced at first hand his growing irrelevance in the formal politics of the country. Thabo Mbeki was then the only deputy president, and it became increasingly obvious that he was going to be Mandela's successor.

But the road of the GNU was riddled with corrugations. Enormous expectations on delivery had been created in the rhetoric of the Freedom Charter and the promises of the 'people's mass liberation movement'. I remember writing a paper in November 1995 with the title 'The GNU Paralyzed by Competing Virtues', in which I made the point that the GNU could not be attacked for doing nothing, but on the contrary for trying to do too much simultaneously without having adequate resources and manpower to do so. I posed the following questions:

- In the tension between democratic practice and stability, how far can unrestrained populism be tolerated? Can nurses, municipal workers, homeless people be allowed to exercise their democratic rights at the expense of the rights of others by preventing health care, trashing public property and invading empty houses?

- In the tension between the imperatives of growth and industrial democracy, what is the correct balance between the democratic rights of workers and policy initiatives to stimulate growth in the economy?

- In the tension between maintaining a human rights culture and transforming the criminal justice system, what are the limits of maintaining law and order?

- In the tension between affirmative action and efficient delivery, how far can one go in sacrificing competence and efficiency for political correctness?

Ten years later (2005) these problems were at the root of the discontent which Thabo Mbeki experienced at the General Congress of the ANC in June 2005. But two reports commissioned by President Mandela – the Ncholo Report on Provincial Government tabled in 1997, and the Presidential Review Commission (the so-called Mpai Report) tabled in 1998, were extremely critical of the slow pace and quality of delivery. By then the RDP was accepted as a failure. Mandela accepted these reports with good grace, and reminded people that 'We had come out of the bushes to govern.'

If anything made travelling over corrugations feel like travelling on a highway, it was the performance, charm and presidency of Mandela. He was the master at exploiting the appropriate moment, making a conciliatory gesture, and persuading the international community that South Africa 'was on its way'. He floated above the battle of delivery like a butterfly. Nobody must underestimate his performance at the Rugby World Cup final in 1995. I was there that day, and saw pot-bellied right-wing fanatics from the deep rural areas weeping when Mandela came up to present the victory cup at the end of the game. This was one of the final blows to exclusive right-wing Afrikaner Nationalism. I saw and heard one of the pot-bellied brigade whisper through his tears: 'That is my President.'

It is impossible for me to convey the significance of that shift in my journey from Dakar to Democracy in South Africa. But when serious democracy began with Thabo Mbeki as the first elected president under the current constitution, no amount of symbolic politics or emotionalism was going to satisfy the demand for effective delivery. This remains Mbeki's challenge until 2009.

APPENDIX 1

A POSSIBLE STRATEGY TO APPLY CONSTITUTIONAL LEVERAGE TOWARDS A NON-RACIAL DEMOCRACY

Dr F van Zyl Slabbert, MP

1 Unless the Government (by means of the State President's Address in Opening Parliament; Notice of Legislation for the 1986 session, as well as the Government's performance during the No-Confidence Debate) gives clear and acceptable indication that it intends restoring freedom of choice on a non-racial, non-ethnic basis for the purposes of participating in the constitutional, social and economic spheres of South Africa, I intend resigning my seat at the end of the No-Confidence Debate. By 'restoring freedom of choice' and 'clear and acceptable indication', I mean repealing the Population Registration Act insofar as it serves to impose involuntary racial and ethnic membership for political, social and economic purposes. It also implies the repeal of all consequential legislation which purely on the basis of race or ethnicity prevents any South African citizen from exercising freedom of choice. By repeal, I also mean that present legislative measures not be substituted by new ones pursuing the same objectives.

2 I do not take the decision to resign lightly. It comes after

62

12 years of complete involvement in Parliamentary politics. Although I was, and still am, totally opposed to the present Tricameral system of Parliament, I urged the PFP to participate in it in order to exploit the possibilities of constitutional change.

I did so with apprehension and reluctantly, because I was convinced that the Tricameral system, in its very conception, structure and implementation, was going to make the politics of negotiation more difficult; would polarize black and white more speedily; and would make violence more attractive to an increasing number of frustrated and disenchanted young black South Africans. The PFP said all this during the 1983 Referendum campaign. Despite my worst fears in this regard being realized, I continued to explore (and at our latest Congress again urged the PFP to do likewise) the possibilities of constitutional change within the structure of the Tricameral Parliament. Thus:

a As often as was convenient and possible, I sought interviews with the State President to discuss the problems of escalating violence and constitutional change.

b I accepted an invitation by the State President to serve on an enlarged Cabinet Committee to explore problems of constitutional development as far as blacks are concerned. After an initial floundering about on its exact status, this Committee appears to be bogged down in its own stagnation.

c I gave evidence to the Cabinet Committee on Black

Constitutional Change (not to be confused with the above).

d I sought out individual Cabinet Ministers and Heads of State Departments to discuss how confrontation can be avoided and a relatively peaceful resolution of our conflict can be achieved.

e Together with other members of my Party, I have sought out black spokesmen and leaders in order to determine the likelihood of negotiation.

f With others, I have tried to establish, with limited success, an extra–Parliamentary forum for cooperation in dismantling Apartheid, i.e. the Convention Alliance.

g I have written countless articles, made innumerable speeches and visited as many interest groups, institutions and organizations as was possible to plead the case for constitutional, rather than violent, change – inside as well as outside my country.

In short, I believe that I, as well as the PFP, have not spared ourselves in trying to explore all possibilities and play a constructive role in promoting the politics of negotiation within the existing Parliamentary structure.

3 In doing this I was, and remain, keenly aware that the pivotal actor, who has to precipitate constitutional change and restore freedom of choice so that South Africans can negotiate a non–racial democratic alternative, MUST

be the Government of the day. It took away freedom of choice constitutionally, only it can restore it in the same manner. Only the Government can legally repeal the laws which will lead to the dismantling of Apartheid and create the climate for negotiating an alternative. This is the major reason why I have sought to engage the Government in every possible manner in order to contribute in some manner towards achieving this objective. Consequently, I have not been as involved in protest and mass politics (both valid and necessary). Even now, in considering what conceivable course of action is still possible, I tend towards possibilities of constitutional leverage rather than other alternatives.

4 Of one thing I am completely convinced. I am not prepared to carry on as before. According to my own light and wisdom I have done whatever can be done with the available opportunities, and to continue as before I would be bluffing myself and others (some who have given substantial financial support) that I was making any significant contribution to the politics of negotiation. In short, I personally am no longer prepared to lead the PFP as the Leader of the Official Opposition in the House of Assembly. It would be presumptuous and arrogant of me to imply that another could not do so and do better, and the Party may decide to place this responsibility on another's shoulders. This person will certainly enjoy my sympathy and whatever assistance I can provide.

There is, however, another way in which I can continue to lead the PFP if it wishes me to. As far as I am

concerned, this is the only avenue left to apply constitutional leverage towards a non-racial democracy.

5 In resigning my seat, I am making a political statement.
(Even should I wish to, I do not think I could quietly
withdraw from active politics and hope that the PFP will
carry on in Parliament as before.) By resigning I am in
effect saying: 'The Tricameral system is a political farce
posing as Parliamentary Government; it is a complete
waste of the taxpayers' money; nothing that has been
done since its implementation could not have been done
more efficiently and with less cost under the old
Constitution. The Government uses it to prevaricate,
obscure, confuse and promote political mediocrities. It
claims that it is only a constitutional point of departure
and not the end of the road. That may be so. However,
it can serve as a new point of departure to extend its
Apartheid logic to other spheres of South African life, or
to end it. So far, the former is the order to the day, rather
than the latter, despite the repeal of some racially dis-
criminatory laws as well as attempts to deregulate the
economy. The limited restoration of choice in these areas
simply highlights the Government's determination to
continue denying such choice for constitutional purposes. This is evident in the nonsensical way in which the
Government persists with the concept of own affairs in
the present constitution as well as extending the same
logic to the Regional Service Councils. Nothing that
the Government has said or done implies anything
other than that a black will participate only as a black,
a Coloured as a Coloured, an Indian as an Indian and a

white as a white, in the political future of this country. This has, and continues to be, the fundamental difference in principle between myself and the Government.

For me, reform means the Government has to dismantle Apartheid by restoring freedom of choice on non-racial, non-ethnic grounds. For the Government, reform means making life as acceptable as possible for those who are not white in those structures where it will not allow freedom of choice on a non-racial, non-ethnic basis, i.e. primarily the Constitution of South Africa. From the concept of Independent Homelands to the Tricameral Parliament, the Constitution of South Africa has been unilaterally designed by this Government on an involuntary racial and ethnic basis. Only those who have been prepared to accept this basis, for whatever reason, have enjoyed the patronage of the State – including the PFP. At the heart of it all lies the ethnic and racial classification of the Population Registration Act. This Act is rejected by the overwhelming majority of all South Africans. Recently, the Human Sciences Research Council published detailed and motivated research demonstrating that this Act lies at the root cause of conflict in our country. I, and the PFP, have tried to make exactly this point over the last 12 years to the Government in as many ways as possible. I have been listened to with either polite indifference, or contempt. The Government remains determined to use this Act and the principle contained in it, as its constitutional point of departure and shows no evidence of diverging from this course. As long as it does not, it cannot and will not really dismantle Apartheid. Therefore, a lot more people will die and suffer needlessly. There appears to be nothing more that I can do to prevent this in my present position, and rather than waste my time and others' by continuing as before, I resign my seat.

6   However, it serves very little purpose to make a political statement and resign without testing the support that one's actions have from those who put one in Parliament in the first place. Whatever the reason, people voted for me in the first place or supported the PFP. I and my Party made no bones about what we were trying to achieve by going to Parliament. Despite the unacceptability of the Population Registration Act and consequential racist legislation, we were determined to use whatever constitutional means at our disposal to bring about the complete dismantling of Apartheid and negotiating a non-racial democratic alternative. By resigning, I am in fact saying to the voters: 'It is pointless to carry on in this way. I have explored the possibilities within that structure to the best of my abilities and am no longer prepared to give it the slightest credibility with my continued presence. However, should the government call a by-election in my constituency, I am willing to stand as a candidate and seek the following mandate:-

a   The Tricameral Parliament is a farce and a waste of taxpayers' money.

b   The Government uses it to waste even more money by creating new unworkable structures. In doing so, it is extending the logic of Apartheid to new structures, rather than destroying it in old ones.

c The vast expanding bureaucracy controlled by Government is leading to the complete ruin of our economy and causing unrest and violence between the people of this land.

d The voters of my constituency have charged me as their elected representative not to return to Parliament until the Government clearly commits itself to restoring freedom of choice by dismantling Apartheid completely. This means that all laws will have to be abolished from the Statute books that compel any person on racial or ethnic grounds to belong to any group for political, social or economic purposes. This means, in concrete practical terms, that any person, irrespective of race or ethnicity, should be free to look for work where he wishes and is able to; and should be free to support any political organisation and leader he chooses to. Such organisations must be free to operate openly and the leader free to be chosen, provided both, under conditions of voluntary association, do not indulge in subversion or violence.

e Should the Government make such a commitment, I will support and assist it in bringing about constitutional and non-violent change towards a non-racial, democratic alternative to the best of my ability.'

7 Having explored and considered, as best I can, the available constitutional possibilities, the above appears to be the only sensible one remaining, i.e. to play the constitutional game strictly according to its own rules, to win and then refuse participation, simply because the Constitution is not good enough or worth it.

It is, in fact, a last desperate attempt to make constitutional change relevant to the conflicts in our country. Of course, if I do this as an individual and am elected on the above basis, it will largely be of symbolic significance. If I am not elected, the problem resolves itself and the constitutional game makes me redundant.

8 However, if the PFP Caucus acts in the above manner, it will cause a constitutional crisis and could have a galvanizing effect on the whole Tricameral system. Should the PFP Caucus and Party wish to distance themselves from me in the above respect and carry on as before, I will respect this and accept the consequences. If the Caucus and the Party supports this act, I can continue as its Leader, and I believe we move from individual political symbolism to what could be the beginning of *a strategy to apply constitutional leverage towards a non-racial democracy*. There are obviously risks involved and I will return to some of them presently. But first, the strategy:

a A General Election has to be called by the end of 1989. Under the most favourable conditions the PFP could come back holding the balance of power in the House of Assembly. It seems highly unlikely that we will be able to contest seats for the other two Houses with credibility. More likely the Government will tap 'the right-wing threat' to drain away any potential support for us so that we will come back very much as before, with perhaps a few extra seats from Natal.

b Given the consequences of the State of Emergency, I cannot see how we can easily change the mood in the townships and in the Coloured and Indian communities towards participation in the other two Houses. If anything, the mood for participation is likely to worsen.

c The following could be some of the political consequences in white politics when we resign our seats:

   i At the very least, the Government has to hold by-elections in all our seats. This provides a dramatic and sustained opportunity to highlight the constitutional crisis.

   ii It will be a clear and simple test for the quality of our support from the white electorate. If there is a genuine right-wing drift, it should show in a desertion from us, rather than from the white centre.

   iii We tackle the right-wing threat head on, on our own and not the Government's initiative. In effect, we say to the Government and the white voter – 'You have the opportunity to find out what kind of Official Opposition you want – the right wing or us.'

   iv Parliament, the Government will have to deal primarily with the right rather than use us as scapegoats.

   v We clear the decks for a General Election – whether

71

the Government calls one immediately as a result of our actions or holds back until 1989.

d Some of the consequences *outside* the context of white politics would be even more significant:
  i All parties in the Indian and Coloured Houses would immediately experience an intensified crisis of credibility.
  ii It is the only way in which I can see the PFP opening up the possibility of effective participation in a General Election for the other two Houses. Our slogan – Let us call the Bluff.
  iii After such a General Election, the PFP could exert constitutional leverage by having the majority of Indian and Coloured seats and approaching a balance of power in the white House.
  iv It is the only way in which the PFP can make non-racial politics constitutionally relevant under the present circumstances.

e I believe the country and the PFP are in a make-or-break situation and this strategy will force us to the centre of the political debate. We have just completed a fundraising campaign to promote the 'politics of negotiation'. In this way, we can dramatically highlight what real negotiation is about.

9 The risks are as many as the limitation of one's imagination will allow. But most, if not all of them, are present in any case. Consider the following:

a The Government may call a General Election immediately because of our resignation. (It can do so in any case. At least it will be doing so on our initiative and strategy.)

b   The Government may suspend the Constitution. (If it does, we have simply been prolonging the inevitable.)

c   The Government can start a massive propaganda campaign against us. (What's new?)

d   The voters may reject us. (If so, what kind of mandate have we been deluding ourselves with?)

e   We could destroy our base in Parliament. (After three sessions in the Tricameral Parliament, a base for what?)

f   We may lose some of our marginal seats. (This is more likely if we wait passively for the next General Election than if we do something dramatic.)

g   Polarization has gone too far to grab any new initiative in so-called Coloured and Indian communities. (If so, we are wasting our time in any case.)

The **timing** and **execution** of this strategy are important.

a   Timing

    i   Ideally, we should be ready to seize on any appropriate political opportunity to execute this strategy. Unfortunately, we do not have the time to become completely ready.

    ii I believe psychologically and in terms of the politi-
cal calendar, the most strategic time is the end of the
No-Confidence Debate.

b Execution

    i I believe Nic Olivier and the Research Department
should stay on and continue to process questions.

    ii We must try to brief a marketing team as tho-
roughly as possible in order to prepare the most
effective publicity campaign.

    iii Secrecy is of the utmost importance. Consequently,
not only the Government but, unfortunately, many
in the Party will be caught by surprise.

    iv As soon as possible after the resignations, Party
formations will have to be briefed either through
regional meetings or a Federal Congress. In any
case, the PFP will have to give its blessing to the
strategy in some way or the other.

    v Because the campaign will have to be well orches-
trated, some new appropriate Party members will
have to be employed for this purpose.

c I believe, strategically, the country is ready for an
initiative of this kind. It may be the last opportunity
for an Opposition such as ours to precipitate incisive political action. In any case, I prefer to go out
with a bang rather than to whimper along in the
slipstream of the Government's repression and
incompetence.

7 January 1986

APPENDIX II

DAKAR COMMUNIQUÉ

1 A conference organized by IDASA took place in Dakar, Senegal from 9–12 July 1987. Participants were made up of South Africans from inside South Africa of which the majority were Afrikaans-speaking persons, and a delegation from the ANC.

2 His Excellency, President Abdou Diouf, welcomed the participants and gave them exceptional hospitality.

3 The participants from South Africa took part in their individual capacities. They shared a common commitment of having rejected both the ideology and practice of the apartheid system. They were drawn from the academic, professional, cultural, religious and business fields.

4 Although the group represented no organized formation within South Africa, their place within, particularly, the Afrikaans-speaking communities, and the fact that they were meeting with the ANC, invested the conference with an overwhelming atmosphere that this was part of the process of the South African people making history. In similar manner, the international community focused its attention on the conference. Participants could not but be aware that some of the adherents of Apartheid regarded the participation of the group as an

act of betrayal, not only to the Apartheid state, but also to the community of Afrikanerdom.

5 The conference was organized around four principal topics:

a Strategies for bringing about fundamental change in South Africa
b The building of national unity
c Perspectives with regard to the structures of the government of a free South Africa.
d A future economy for South Africa

6 The discussions took place in an atmosphere of cordiality and a unity of purpose arising from a shared commitment towards the removal of the Apartheid system and the building of a united, democratic and a non-racial South Africa.

7 The group listened to and closely questioned the perspectives, goals, strategy and tactics of the ANC. The main areas of concern arose over the ANC's resolve to maintain and intensify the armed struggle. While the group accepted the historical reality of the armed struggle, although not all could support it, they were deeply concerned over the proliferation of uncontrolled violence.

However, all participants recognized that the source of violence in South Africa derives from the fact that the use of force is fundamental to the existence and practice of racial domination. The group developed an understanding of the conditions which have generated a widespread revolt of the black people and the deep resolve of the ANC.

8 Conference unanimously expressed preference for a negotiated resolution of the South African question. Participants recognized that the attitude of those in power in South Africa is the principle obstacle to progress in this regard. It was further accepted that the unconditional release of all political prisoners and the unbanning of organizations is a fundamental prerequisite for such negotiations to take place.

9 Proceeding from the common basis that there is an urgent necessity to realize the goal of a non-racial democracy, participants agreed that they all have an obligation to act for the achievement of this objective. They accepted that different strategies must be used in accordance with the possibilities available to the various forces opposed to the system of Apartheid. They accepted that in its conduct, this struggle must assist in the furtherance both of democratic practice and in the building of a nation of all South Africans, black and white.

10 It was accepted between the two delegations that further contacts of this nature were necessary. Equally, it was important that such contacts should involve more and wider sections of the South African people in order to dispel misunderstanding and fear and to reinforce the broad democratic movement.

11 Conference expressed profound appreciation to His Excellency, President Abdou Diouf, the Government and people of Senegal for the warm welcome extended to the delegates, as well as the assistance afforded to them to ensure the success of the conference. It further expressed gratitude to Madam Danielle Mitterrand for her assistance in organizing the conference and extended thanks to all other governments and individuals who contributed material resources to make the conference possible.

APPENDIX III

THE DELEGATES WHO ATTENDED
THE DAKAR CONFERENCE

1. Those who came from inside South Africa

Max du Preez started and became editor of *Vrye Weekblad*, which became a thorn in the flesh of the governing establishment by exposing corruption and 'third force' activities. He was later joined by Hennie Serfontein, doyen of Afrikaner investigative journalists, who also made a documentary which included the Dakar Conference called 'Breaking the Fetters'.

Lawrence Schlemmer – arguably one of the best and most uncompromising social researchers, who became Deputy Director of the HSRC.

Hermann Giliomee, professor of Political Science at UCT and one-time editor of *Die Suid-Afrikaan*, continued through columns in newspapers and magazines to address particularly Afrikaners about the need for fundamental change.

André du Toit, professor of Political Science at UCT, one of the most incisive political scientists in South Africa, also editor of *Die Suid-Afrikaan* and board member of IDASA. Hardy Botha (artist) started a non-racial and open artists' colony/community at Daljosafat.

Jannie Gagiano, political scientist at Stellenbosch University; a totally uncompromising intellect who continues unchecked with his anarchistic destabilising of hallowed paradigms.

Manie van Rensburg, film director, who came back and under impossible circumstances managed to produce 'Taxi to Soweto' and 'The Native Who Caused all the Trouble'.

André Brink did more of what he has always done, resisting intolerance and authoritarianism through writing and lecturing.

Breyten Breytenbach continued as an unreconstructed rebel, discovering and inventing causes which could undermine and expose corrupt authority anywhere, any place.

Jakes Gerwel now chairs the Board of Trustees of the Nelson Mandela Foundation.

Jaap du Randt succeeded Jakes Gerwel as Rector of UWC.

Franklin Sonn, head of the Peninsula Technikon, joined the ANC and fought in their Western Cape election campaign, and became South African ambassador to the USA.

Randall van der Heever became secretary general of SADTU (South African Democratic Teachers' Union) and is now an MP for the ANC.

Theuns Eloff resigned as a 'Dopper Dominee' and headed up the Consultative Business Movement, and later co-orchestrated CODESA, Multi-Party Forum and TEC Secretariat.

Beyers Naudé continued being Beyers Naudé and was part of the first ANC delegation which signed the Groote Schuur Minute.

Chris Louw, journalist, edited *Die Suid-Afrikaan* and was political correspondent for the *Mail & Guardian*.

Revel Fox, doyen of architects, influenced the younger generation in appreciating their living space.

Leon Louw, head of the Free Market Foundation, continued to promote the goals of a 'free market' and 'liberty'.

Adie Enthoven works with me on the Witwatersrand Metropolitan Chamber.

Marina de Beer, lecturer in Afrikaans literature and active in gender issues.

Trudie de Ridder was disowned by her family and fired from her job as educational psychologist for going to Dakar.

Grethe Fox became active in cultural organisations to promote non-racial arts, and like her husband (Manie van Rensburg) suffered ostracism from the establishment.

Michael Savage, professor of Sociology at UCT and currently seconded to the Open Society Foundation as Executive Director.

Braam Viljoen, professor of Theology and brother of Constand Viljoen, worked tirelessly to promote negotiations between his brother and the ANC.

Tommy Bedford, architect, former Springbok rugby captain, with his uncle, Sir Laurens van der Post, tried to influence Inkatha and Buthelezi.

Andrew Savage, businessman and MP, until his death did magnificent work in the townships of Port Elizabeth and started the Human Rights Trust.

Alex Boraine, executive director of IDASA, after Dakar arranged many seminars, conferences and workshops inside and outside South Africa on democracy in a future South Africa.

Peter Gastrow, DP MP, headed up the Natal Peace Accord and chaired the Justice Sub-Committee of the TEC.

EK Moorcroft, DP MP, is very active in agricultural reform and land affairs.

Pierre Cronje, one of the first DP MPs to resign and join the ANC, and who worked for them in the Natal Midlands.

André Odendaal, professor of History at UWC, openly worked for the ANC on his return.

Johan van der Westhuizen, professor of Human Rights Law at the University of Pretoria, who played an active role in promoting discussion and work on human rights in Pretoria.

Gerhard Erasmus, professor of Law, University of Stellenbosch, part of drafting committee of experts for both the Namibian and South African constitutions.

2. Honorary South Africans from outside

Heribert Adam, professor of Sociology at Simon Fraser University, an authority on South African political dynamics, after Dakar produced a number of books on the folly of continued domination, including *The Negotiated Revolution*.

Theo Hanf, director of the Arnold Bergstraesser Institute, produced the first comprehensive research survey of South Africa in 1977, titled 'South Africa – The Prospects for Peaceful Change', is currently finalising a survey, and was head of the European Missions Section on voter education during the elections.

Baron Klaus von der Ropp, an 'honorary Afrikaner' who calls himself 'Die Woestynman' because he lost himself in the Namib Desert. He was a European Mission Observer during the elections, and was particularly helpful in finding funds to promote dialogue between Constand Viljoen and the ANC.

Hans Cristoph Buch, German author, Berlin.

3. Those who were in exile

The following, with the positions they held after the 1994 elections:

Thabo Mbeki – Deputy Vice President of South Africa (now President)

Alfred Nzo – Minister of Foreign Affairs

Steve Tshwete – Minister of Sport

Mac Maharaj – Minister of Transport

Pallo Jordan – Minister of Posts, Telecommunications and Broadcasting

Kader Asmal – Minister of Water Affairs and Forestry

Penuel Maduna – Deputy Minister of Home Affairs

Bridget Mabandla and Essop Pahad – MPs for the ANC

Barbara Masekela – personal assistant to President Mandela in Shell House, and master of ceremonies for the inauguration at the Union Buildings.

CHAPTER 3

BACKROOM FACTOTUM AND FACILITATOR

The Goree Institute

Ever since the Dakar Conference in 1987, Breyten Brey-tenbach and I tried to find an answer to President Abdou Diouf's question: 'And now, what next?' He was insistent that the Dakar Conference could not be a one-off event and that there had to be some sustained follow-up. Breyten and I had visited Dakar a few times since 1987, exploring a few possibilities.

I had also in the mean time become involved with the African Leadership Forum of General Olusegun Obasanjo of Nigeria. He had been a member of the Eminent Persons Group that visited Mandela in prison during PW Botha's era, and was also a former head of state of Nigeria – in fact, the first military ruler who restored civilian rule in Nigeria. I found him to be an extremely affable, shrewd politician. He invited me to African Leadership Forum meetings in Addis Ababa, Lagos and Windhoek. These were more in the nature of workshops attended by current or former African leaders or politicians. What struck me was the desperate need for this kind of interaction, not only on the leadership level, but at a younger, NGO level. African countries needed to compare their resources, and problems of economic development and political transformation, with one another: the pitfalls to be avoided, and how regional cooperation could be promoted. Breyten agreed with all of this, but added that the cultural dimension, particularly in the African context, was important. Not only had African countries experienced French, British, German, Portuguese and Belgian colonialisation, but indigenous cultures responded in different ways to the social, economic and political impact of such influences. We then decided we should canvass support for the creation of an Institute for Democracy, Development and Culture in Africa. We wanted this institute to be on Goree Island, to also symbolise the movement from slavery to democracy, and it should try to provide sabbatical facilities for scholars, researchers, authors, bureaucrats and politicians to come and write up their work and compare notes with one another. It also had to arrange workshops and seminars to which delegates from across Africa and Africanists outside Africa could come.

Breyten and I went to see President Diouf about the idea, and he was very excited and enthusiastic. We emphasised the importance of the autonomy of such an Institute and he agreed, saying that it would have diplomatic immunity and that an Accord de Siège between his government and the Institute would be drawn up.

My daughter, Tania, had graduated in languages at UCT, and after travelling through Europe for a few years ended up in Dakar. She had been working there for a year when Breyten and I decided on a year-long feasibility study to see if the Institute would fly. André Zaaiman, who had been a director of IDASA in Pretoria, made himself available to be project director of the feasibility study. Tania, being fluent in French, was the liaison person assisting Zaaiman, who at that stage could not speak French. Both of them worked extremely hard. Zaaiman became reasonably fluent in French after eight months, and my daughter went back to South Africa.

On 25 June 1991 the Goree Institute was launched. Our building was a restored historical house called the Maison du Soudan. The German embassy had restored it, and in terms of the Accord de Siège the Senegalese government gave it to the Goree Institute to use as its headquarters and conference facility. President Diouf officially opened it. The first Board of Trustees had representatives from Nigeria, Benin, Zambia, Ghana, Senegal, Eritrea, South Africa, Canada, Germany and France. I was elected its first president, and Zaaiman became executive director. Our first workshop was on Democratic Transition in Africa, and in attendance were scholars from the USA, Latin America, Eastern Europe and Africa. Breyten had also arranged another workshop between European and African poets, and we had puppeteers from Mali dancing at our official opening of the Maison du Soudan.

Initially the Goree Institute was desperately strapped for cash. We needed seed money until Breyten and I could go fundraising. I wrote to Soros in New York, whom I had not spoken to for three years. It was a long letter, setting out the reason for the Institute. His reply was one sentence: 'It gives me pleasure to contribute $50 000 towards the establishment of the Goree Institute.' We then had a reasonably successful fundraising campaign, and the Institute was up and running.

Maison du Soudan was appropriated by the state, and our workers forcefully removed; and we had to find alternative conference facilities and offices for our staff. Breyten was acting executive director from 2002 to 2005, and did sterling work. After 14 years, the Goree Institute for Democracy, Development and Culture is still running. In January 2005 a very successful workshop was run on Electoral Reform in Africa, attended by representatives from 17 African countries.

There have also been extraordinary, even bizarre incidents. One of them involved Obasanjo, Abacha and Ken Saro-Wiwa of Nigeria, the Goree Institute, and then-deputy president Thabo Mbeki.

On 10 November 1995, Abacha, dictator of Nigeria, hanged the poet Ken Saro-Wiwa (Obasanjo had been imprisoned without trial by Abacha). Nelson Mandela, as president of South Africa, was in New Zealand at the time of the hanging, and issued a vitriolic attack condemning Abacha. He described the Abacha regime as 'an illegitimate, barbaric, arrogant military dictatorship which has murdered activists using a kangaroo court and false evidence.' The Goree Institute immediately arranged a meeting of all opposition groups in Nigeria. During the meeting Zaaiman came to me and said that Mbeki would like to see me back in South Africa with the list of attendees.

A few weeks later, I sat in Mbeki's office. I gave him the list and he looked at it and said dismissively, 'Oh, a bunch of Yorubas.' I asked him, 'Are you not incensed at Saro-Wiwa's execution and Obasanjo's incarceration?' He went into a long-winded explanation, saying he was ANC representative in Lagos when Abacha was an up-and-coming officer; Abacha was a complex man and had to be handled 'carefully'. It was clear to me that he was embarrassed by Mandela's reaction. I asked, 'Are you not going to push for Obasanjo's release?' He said it was very difficult. If Abacha released Obasanjo he would also have to release Abiola and the Fulani Housa, Yaraduar. The latter was 'a real revolutionary and a danger to Abacha'. I subsequently found out that Yaraduar's uncle fathered Abacha's wife's first child, and there was more personal animosity than fear involved. (In any case, Abacha copulated himself to extinction with two Indian prostitutes and an overdose of Viagra.) Abiola and Yaraduar died in prison. Obasanjo came out and became president of Nigeria once again. He and Mbeki laugh and hug each other at AU meetings. What the Goree Institute taught me, amongst many other things: I do not need Anglo-Africans to come and sermonise me about what it means to be 'an African'. They can all go and suck eggs!

The Metropolitan Chamber

In March 1991 I was approached by the Administrator of the Transvaal, Danie Hough, and asked whether I would consider being chairman of the Central Witwatersrand Metropolitan Chamber (MC). This was a negotiating forum which had come about as a result of prolonged bargaining between the TPA (Transvaal Provincial Administration) led by Olaus van Zyl, and the Soweto People's Delegation led by Cyril Ramaphosa. The purpose of the MC was to improve the quality of services for the people of Greater Soweto by establishing a common tax base, and to negotiate new non-racial democratic structures of local/metropolitan government. (Of course, according to Essop Pahad and Willie Esterhuyse, Thabo Mbeki had already negotiated the necessary concessions from 'the regime' by September 1989.)

From the MC I learned a great deal about the very practical problems confronting our democratic transition. If ever one wanted to come face to face with how bruised and battered our civil society had become through years of apartheid rule, then the MC was as good a vantage point from which to do so as any. I also saw first-hand how sound local democratic practice is linked to immediate problems concerning the daily quality of life – water, sewerage, electricity, refuse removal, housing, transport, etc. Lofty pronouncements about the virtues of citizenship in a new democratic constitution will fall on deaf ears if these problems are not attended to at the local level.

At the heart of the problem with which the MC grappled was the legacy of White and Black cities/towns/suburbs lying next to each other with highly unequal infrastructures, yet complete economic interdependence. To talk about a democratic South Africa without addressing this kind of inequality at the local residential/commercial/industrial level and the kind of political structures that would be appropriate, is simply self-delusion. Politically the 'new South Africa' is going to survive or go under in its cities, and I do not for one moment underestimate the very serious problems of rural underdevelopment, poverty and neglect. But the political powder kegs lie in our cities.

The MC had to try and break the rent and rate boy-cott brought about by the so-called Koornhof Bills that accompanied the Tricameral Constitution. The 'urban Blacks' were offered limited local self-government as a sop to losing citizenship at the central level. This promptly led to a rent and rate boycott, and the attempts to make the townships 'ungovernable'. The MC was the instrument created to help break the impasse. It enabled me to move around in places like Kliptown, Chicken Farm, Dube and Westbury, and to experience first-hand the slow break-down of services and people's determination not to pay for them. The refrain was, 'We'll pay when we have legiti-mate leaders.' I knew then it was not going to be that simple. The fact was that people had become used to not paying. I remember standing in the kitchen of a young mother in Westbury and noticed a fridge, washing machine and stove. She said she did not like the new sys-tem. In this case it was a coupon system, and one could see on the meter how power was being consumed. I asked her why. She said, 'The old system was better because we did not have to pay.' It became clear to me that there were three categories of potential rate-payers in this metro-politan area, and I'm sure in others as well: those who cannot pay; those who can, but won't; and those who can and do. How to computerise these categories is unclear to me. But this will be compounded many times over if there are not competent debt-collectors. What I also realised very clearly was that no degree of democratic involve-ment could automatically provide technical competence. Then and now, I have no idea how to provide the proper reticulation of water supply or electric power. Technicians who can do things like these are vital for effective delivery of services.

On 9 December 1993 the MC finally reached an inclusive agreement to end rent and rates boycotts in the Greater Soweto Area; not a moment too soon, as basic services were on the point of collapse and money was running out fast. I had been chairman of the Chamber for two-and-a-half years, and during that time the membership of the Chamber had been increased from civic associations to include members from the ANC/SACP, Black city councillors, some from the Sofasonke Party, and members from the NP and DP. In fact it included all political parties in the region with the exception of the Conservative Party, who did not want to participate. The life of the MC came to an end early in 1994, and it was transformed into a Metropolitan Negotiating Forum to assist with local and metropolitan elections, and transformation. Local transition cannot be a precondition for national transition, but it will certainly determine to what extent we have been successful. It is also the area in which Black aspirations and White fears form the pit-face of change.

The SABC Board

I was driving back from a weekend in Swaziland in the middle of 1993 when I heard over the car radio that I had been appointed chairman of the new SABC board. To say that I was stunned would be an understatement. I knew that I had been nominated as a member and was on the shortlist. I immediately issued a statement over the car phone through Jenny Nothard, my secretary, rejecting the appointment, saying that I felt embarrassed and had not been consulted.

When I subsequently heard of the circumstances which led to my appointment, my embarrassment turned to anger. The panel of learned judges had recommended Prof. Njabulo Ndebele as chairman and myself as deputy chairman. De Klerk found this unacceptable, and bargained with the judges to get me appointed as chairman and Prof. Ivy Matsepe-Casaburri as deputy chairperson. Never at any stage did any of them consider the possibility that the Board itself should appoint its office-bearers. The manner in which the whole thing had been dealt with caused a political furore. Through no action on my part, I ended up as the proverbial meat in the political sandwich — everyone wanted to have a bite at me. De Klerk wanted me as chairman, Mandela made it quite clear he did not want me as chairman (this was after frank personal discussions with both). The Campaign for Independent Broadcasting (CIB — Raymond Louw, Allister Sparks, etc.), a special interest lobby concerned with the state of public broadcasting in South Africa, made it quite clear that 'my integrity' was under threat because I would be seen as 'De Klerk's appointee'. (Funnily enough, they never showed the same concern about the integrity of Dr Matsepe-Casaburri, who was in exactly the same position as myself in this regard, and who subsequently became chairperson when I resigned.)

When I reached home later after the drive from Swaziland, I had a call from Pallo Jordan. 'Van, for your sake, get off.' Mandela: 'My boy, you're doing great work on the

MC, don't destroy your reputation.' From De Klerk: 'Please come and see me urgently in Cape Town.' I said to him, 'How can you appoint me without consulting me?' He said, 'I could not get hold of you.' I said, 'Bullshit.'

In his Cape Town office he asked me to please call the first meeting so that the Board could at least be constituted. At the first Board meeting I duly 'constituted' the Board and tendered my resignation. The Board unanimously (i.e. ANC members included) asked me to stay on for a few weeks to help the Board find its feet. My intention was to resign immediately, but they persuaded me to carry on for a few weeks. This was obviously a mistake. In my dealings with De Klerk and Mandela on how to sort out the mess, I concluded that the last thing on their minds was the 'independence of the SABC Board'. The issue was simple: power and control. If neither of them could get it as far as the Board was concerned, they would both fight tooth and nail to prevent the other from getting it. I was simply incidental to the fight, and was going to be the first casualty.

While I was at a workshop on Goree from 20-23 June 1993 I received a fax from a concerned Adv Fikile Bam, a friend and fellow Board member, who informed me that at a clandestine meeting between some Board members and representatives of the CIB, a strategy had been discussed to get rid of me as current chairman and to get the original recommendations of the panel of judges reinstated. As far as I was concerned, they were leaning on an open door. I did, however, tick the names of Raymond Louw and Allister Sparks into my memory file. They had never even bothered to pick up the phone to ask me my own opinion – something they often did when I was still in party politics.

The special meeting was held at the request of Prof Fatima Meer, a fellow Board member. I had known her for many years, and from time to time she displayed a remarkable ability to formulate her prejudices at such a level of abstraction that she managed to accommodate all contradictions when pleading the case for the current establishment of her choice.

On my return from the Goree workshop, I immediately called an emergency Board meeting. Fatima Meer made it quite clear that whatever contribution I had made to democratisation in South Africa as 'a White Afrikaner male', 'the people' would not tolerate me in that position. As far as I was concerned this kind of logic informs ethnic cleansing. I told the Board I could not stay on any longer as *they* had requested, and resigned as chairman immediately. A few weeks later I resigned from the Board altogether.

I learned the following: Mandela did not want me because I was not 'a loyal servant of the ANC' and I was a 'White Afrikaner male'. De Klerk wanted me because I was not a 'loyal servant of the ANC' and was 'a White Afrikaner male'. A few days after my resignation Mandela phoned me and thanked and congratulated me for my 'patriotic act'.

Co-chairperson of the Local Government Electoral Task Team (LGETT)

In early 1995 I was approached by Roelf Meyer, then minister of constitutional development, and Valli Moosa, deputy minister, and asked whether I would co-chair with Khehla Shubane a task team to oversee the first local government elections. I agreed, and a meeting was held of representatives from all the local governments in the country (680) in Johannesburg on 14 March 1995, at which I said the following:

HOW CAN OUR LOCAL GOVERNMENT ELECTIONS BE A SUCCESS?

1 If we are to have successful elections, and I certainly believe this to be possible, then it will most certainly depend on the people gathered here today.

We have central government which provided the constitutional framework within which the elections have to take place and keep an eye on the funding.

We have regional governments which have the statutory or legal authority to see to it that the elections take place. In effect, in each region, the regional government fulfils the same role as the IEC did for the national elections – it proclaims interim arrangements for local government; oversees the demarcation of boundaries; and processes requests for funding.

Finally, we have the appointed representatives of the emerging local government bodies, such as Transitional Metropolitan Councils and Transitional Local Councils.

It is at this level where appointed bodies have to be converted into elected bodies, and where the actual implementation of local government elections will take place.

2 All of us together have an enormous responsibility to make the people of this country aware of the five key issues which are central to the success of these elections. What are they?

   a Africa cannot stop its process of democratization by it not holding successful local government elections. We will be the laughing stock of the world if we continue to boast about how successfully we managed national and regional elections but we simply ignore local elections. In effect, we will be saying we want a democratic national and regional government, but where we live and experience the quality of life every day, we literally don't care what kind of government we have. It is the duty of all South Africans to help to complete our process of democratization by holding successful local government elections. It is necessary to bring democracy into the community.

   b We must use every opportunity to explain and demonstrate to people why the local elections are fundamentally different to national and regional elections. They are fundamentally different in both form and substance. As far as *form* is concerned: *last* year people voted for a party on one ballot paper at the nearest polling booth with a wide range of identification documents; *this* year, people vote for persons who will represent wards, as well as for parties, and they will do so at predetermined polling booths where their names will appear on a voters' roll.

They can only appear on that voters' roll if they have registered using a South African Identity Document, and they will cast their vote on more than one ballot paper – one with names of actual candidates, and another with the names of parties contesting for support.

But, these elections differ fundamentally also in *substance* from last year's elections. *Last year's* election settled the problem of legitimacy of the Constitution and Government at national and regional level. *This year's* elections are far more involved with the problems of delivery of basic services which we depend on or need in our daily lives. We do not only have to legitimatize and stabilize local government by having democratic elections, but these local governments have to provide and improve the quality of basic services such as water, sewerage, refuse removal, electricity, etc. There are not national or regional departments to provide these absolutely essential services for each local community.

c   From the above, it follows that successful registration is an absolute pre-condition for successful elections. We can accept that *low registration* will lead to *high instability* on the day of the elections, and this in turn will compound problems of legitimacy for the new incoming elected local government. I would rather have a 30% poll on a voters' roll which represents 70%

of the voters, than a 60% poll which only represents 30% of the voters. In the former case, people were entitled to vote, but they did not, so they deserve the government they get. In the latter case, we can never know how many people wanted to vote but could not because they were not registered. We have to overcome people's fear, apathy and pre-judice and get them to register. Registration is not only necessary to produce a voters' roll for these elections, but for all future elections. An up-to-date voters' roll is the foundation of all future democratic elections. However, particularly for local elections based on a ward system, a voters' roll is absolutely essential to make sure that local people vote for local representatives.

d If we understand how critically important registration is for an up-to-date voters' roll, then all of us here must realize and act upon the fact, that registration itself is primarily a local and regional responsibility. There is no national task force taking charge of registration. When people ask me: 'Can the Task Group on Local government Elections register the people in time?' I reply: 'No!' 'Why?' Because it is not our task to register anybody. We must assist in coordinating the registrations and the overall process of the elections, but voters have to be registered by either themselves or by interested parties at the local/regional level assisting them. You cannot wish to be an elected representative of our local government body and come to me and say: 'People don't understand why they must register.' If you want their vote *you* have to explain to them why they must register. If you can't, then you don't even understand how you yourself wish to get elected. Yes, it is the responsibility of the voter to register, but if we are to have successful registration, then at the local level, parties and NGOs must drive the process. It is quite possible, and there are many instances to prove this, where large national parties lose local elections because smaller parties and independent candidates were more successful in registering their own supporters.

e When I said that these local elections are locally driven, I mean they are locally driven in every respect. You at the local level will determine the number of voting stations, scrutinize the candidates who present themselves for election, engage in voter education and communication, and motivate requests for funding. How energetically and disciplined you do this will have a fundamental bearing on the success of your own elections. In the final analysis, one regional government cannot monitor the elections for another region, and one local community cannot do so for another. The government you elect at the local level is the one you will have worked for, or not.

3 Let me place the importance of these elections in a broader context. A lot of people are impatient because they feel the pace of change is too slow. They feel that they have voted for a national/regional government and now they wish to see things happen. But ask yourself a

few simple questions: *As a resident* in a community: where does water come out of a tap; where do sewerage systems work; where is garbage removed; where does electricity provide light and energy? If I have these services they are in my house. If I do not, that is where I want them. But ask yourself as a *builder in the community* – where do I get permission to build on land; who determines the building standards; who will guarantee the provision of basic services for potential home dwellers? There is no national/regional government who looks after this. It has to happen at the local level. Ask yourself as a normal *member of a community dependent on community services*, who looks after street lights, cemeteries, playgrounds, sports fields, etc.?

What is the central point I am making? In whichever way we look at it, we will measure the success of our transition by the demonstrable improvement in the quality of life at the local level. That is where we live every day. In 1999 when we vote again for a national government, the average voter will ask simple questions to determine whether things have really improved and got better for him or her. Do I feel safer and more secure when I walk from the taxi to my house after work? Are the streets cleaner, and do the street lights work? Are my children safe playing in the street? Am I in a better house or neighbourhood than last time?

Let me put it quite bluntly to you – successful transformation, effective implementation of the projects of the RDP are held hostage to the absence of a stable local government in our country. The longer we delay bringing democratic stability to our local governments, the longer the delay of development projects, the faster the decline in basic standards of living, and the more political anger and impatience will be generated.

Let me conclude by making a fairly certain prediction. When we as South Africans look back at the end of this century, which is only a few years away, we will measure our success as a nation, not by brilliant speeches in our political assemblies, nor by the actions of individuals, statesmen or politicians, great as they may be. We will measure our success by how Johannesburg and Soweto, Pretoria and Mamelodi, East London and Mdantsane, Port Elizabeth and New Brighton, Cape Town and Khayelitsha, Durban and KwaMashu began to build a genuinely new South Africa at the local level, where we live our daily lives. A critical first step will be the forthcoming local elections, and each one of you here today is vital for the success of those elections.

The task team soon discovered it had taken on an enormous job. We visited as many local councils as we could, particularly where we anticipated some difficulties. A few incidents stand out.

The elections had to be performed according to the prescriptions of the Local Government Transition Act. This was an extraordinarily incompetent and clumsy piece of legislation. With our executive we drafted about eighty amendments and made an appointment to see President Mandela. We urged him to give effect to these amendments. He asked, 'How?' We said, 'By decree,' as the amendments were not of any major constitutional consequence. He was a bit unsure, but agreed. The moment his amendments were made public, the NP reported him to the Constitutional Court saying that the president had acted unconstitutionally. The Court agreed, and President Mandela had to withdraw his decrees and have the Act properly amended in parliament. This was duly done, and the LGETT could proceed with its work in terms of the amended Act. This was the first ruling of the Constitutional Court, and the first ruling against the president of the country. President Mandela accepted the ruling with good grace, and I believe South Africa passed an important milestone as far as the independence of the judiciary is concerned.

The second incident was typical of many small-town municipalities. I was talking to the town clerk of Carolina about the forthcoming local elections. Eventually, ashen-faced, he asked, 'Do you know what you are doing to me and Carolina? I have a declining revenue base that can barely provide proper services for the Whites, now you want me to provide the same quality of services for Whites, Indians and Blacks! It can't be done. It's bad enough that Whites think that services will decline. But Blacks and Indians think services will improve for everybody to the same level that Whites enjoyed.' I just said to him, 'Welcome to the new South Africa.' There is a large Indian population in Carolina, and they lived in a group area called 'Carolindia'. Needless to say, Carolindia no longer exists.

The third issue involved local government elections in KwaZulu-Natal. There was fierce competition between ANC and Inkatha, and a lot of reports about irregularities. This was typified by the hostility between an Inkatha warlord, David Ntombela, and an ANC warlord, Sifiso Nkabinde. Both operated in the Natal Midlands area, and each proclaimed his area as a 'no-go' area for the other. When I asked Nkabinde why there were no other parties contesting in his area he said, 'Because I am too popular!' When I asked the same question of Ntombela he said, 'Why should there be?' Things were so unsettled in Natal that local government elections had to be postponed to 1996. After the elections in Natal, Sefiso Nkabinde joined Bantu Holomisa's UDM and was assassinated shortly afterwards. Tough environment, KwaZulu-Natal.

Finally, after all the local government elections were held and proclaimed 'reasonably fair and free', Valli Moosa, who succeeded Roelf Meyer as minister of constitutional affairs, conducted an audit of all the local government councils in the country to determine their capacity to survive. He concluded that one-third would go under, one-third needed assistance in order to survive, and one-third could make it on their own. This assessment finally led to the restructuring of local governments from 680 to the $\pm$ 250 we have today. This is still the level at which the success of South Africa's democracy will be measured in the most concrete way.

Chairing the Cabinet Committee Task Team Investigating Alternative Electoral Systems

I tabled the Electoral Task Team report to the cabinet in March 2003. In all my experience as a factotum/facilitator I had never felt so used, abused and insulted. It started off badly and ended worse. Chief Mangosuthu Buthelezi, in his capacity as minister of home affairs, approached me in early 2001 and said that the cabinet had unanimously agreed that

I should chair the task team. I said to him, 'Are you sure, and do you really think the ANC is serious about exploring alternatives?' He said that with the certification of the Constitution by the Constitutional Court in 1996 the finalisation of the electoral system had been postponed, and now had to be looked at as a matter or urgency.

I waited one year for my letter of appointment. President Mbeki, in that period, when asked how the ETT was coming on, replied in parliament that it 'was doing fine' and was being chaired by Dr van Zyl Slabbert. By then Buthelezi was almost apoplectic with frustration, and was convinced that the delay in my appointment was done deliberately to humiliate him.

I made an appointment with Deputy President Jacob Zuma with whom I was on friendly terms. I said to him that the situation was becoming totally ridiculous and untenable, and that I was no longer available. 'Good God, no. You can't. We will look like Mugabe.' I said to him that if within two weeks I did not get a letter of appointment, I was out.

And so, a year after I was approached, the ETT got off the ground. At the very first meeting of the ETT most of the representatives from the IEC (Independent Electoral Commission) more or less made it clear that the ETT exercise was a waste of time, and that the current system should remain. I said, if this was the prevailing view 'Let's close shop and go home.' The majority, however, felt we should at least explore alternatives.

I raised funds from the Konrad Adenauer Foundation, the Danes and DIFID (the British). The whole exercise did not cost the South African taxpayer one cent, even though it was a cabinet committee. With the money from the Konrad

Adenauer Foundation a two-day workshop was held in September 2002, which international and local experts attended. Johnny de Lange, ANC MP, also came along and could hardly contain his contempt for the work of the ETT.

We then listened to representations from all the parties in Parliament, and finally I decided the whole exercise was a waste of time and money. Although the majority on the ETT proposed a multi-member constituency system, it was made quite clear to me, after discussions with Kader Asmal and Essop Pahad, and a call from an ANC Electoral Committee official, that the government preferred the status quo. During this time the Constitutional Court validated floor-crossing. In their original certification they argued that floor-crossing combined with a closed proportional list system was 'inappropriate and immoral'. Now when the ANC looked favourably upon it, having strongly opposed it, the Constitutional Court found that floor-crossing was not 'unconstitutional'. The ANC suddenly looked favourably upon floor-crossing because it would assist it to capture the Western Cape and KwaZulu-Natal.

I tabled the report with the majority and minority recommendations, as well as the proceedings of the two-day workshop. Apparently Kader Asmal, when discussing the report in cabinet, said that the proceedings should not be contained in the report because they were only included 'to make the Report look bulky'. A friend on the cabinet, not Buthelezi, told me that the report was not read or studied by anybody he could recall.

All in all, a disgusting and eminently forgettable experience, except for the excellent contributions of some of my colleagues, for example:

Norman du Plessis from the IEC whom I regard as an expert of international repute on electoral systems, and who constructed the system of multiple-membership proportional representation; Prof. Glenda Fick, a legal scholar from Wits who went through the whole certification process of 1996 in meticulous fashion; and Prof. Jurgen Elkit from Denmark, another renowned expert on electoral systems, who was part of the first IEC for the 1994 elections. However, I felt for all my colleagues, and was angry at how I was abused and at how I wasted their time.

Aardklop (2002)

In the beginning of 2002, JP Landman, a friend, competent economist and political commentator, asked me to chair Aardklop. Nothing could have been further from my mind. Aardklop is an annual cultural festival within the Afrikaans-speaking language community, and is held in Potchefstroom in the North-West Province.

The very fact that I was approached to chair it is symptomatic of the disintegration of old-style Afrikaner Nationalist cultural institutions and supporting bodies. Aardklop is also symptomatic of a desire felt by still predominantly White, Afrikaans-speaking people to embrace the 'new South Africa' and explore new ventures with other members of the same language community. It is often forgotten that Afrikaans is the third-largest home language spoken by South Africans, approximately 14%, and that the majority of those who speak it are not classified 'White' as in the old Population Registration Act.

One just has to travel through the North-West and Eastern Cape provinces to experience this first-hand.

I remember during the first democratic local government elections, at a meeting in Upington, Valli Moosa, then deputy minister of constitutional affairs, addressing a meeting of about four hundred people. He started off in English, and was interrupted by a Black man speaking to me in Afrikaans and asking whether I would translate the minister's message into Afrikaans as they did not understand a word he was saying.

I accepted the position of chair of Aardklop, making it quite clear it would only be for two years. It was a very interesting two years. The disappearance of an Afrikaner Nationalist governing establishment has unleashed a wide diversity of responses within the Afrikaans language community. It varies from children or even grandchildren of the old establishment who are overcome with a sense of guilt and/or shame and will have nothing to do with any attempt to maintain or promote Afrikaans as one of the 11 official languages of the new South Africa; to former Nationalist Party cabinet members who have sent their children to Australia and 'give feathers' about Afrikaans, as one of them told me; to desperate attempts to revive old-fashioned Afrikaner Nationalism. I suppose Aardklop can be seen as an attempt to show that Afrikaans can be part of 'high culture', 'cool' or fashionable for the young (words like 'cunt', 'fuck' and 'shit' figure prominently in lyrics), and to accommodate the poor and previously disadvantaged. One comes across all of these during the week-long festival. And those who were previously discriminated against attend, and rub salt into the wounds of the guilty.

One of the consequences during my time at Aardklop was the creation of the Sol Plaatje Academy. This is a weekly discussion forum on KykNet, an Afrikaans TV network, on a wide range of current topics. It turned out to be quite popular. Sol Plaatje was one of the founding members of the ANC, and was a multilingual activist in the Potchefstroom area and its surrounds during the early part of the 20th century.

Whether my association with Aardklop and the Sol Plaatje Academy was the precipitant or not, I am not sure, but suddenly over the period 2002-2005 I was approached by a number of organisations that were previously very much part of the old establishment and were interested in what I had to say. A member of the local branch of the Broederbond in Polokwane approached me after a school reunion function in 2003 and asked me whether I would come and talk to them. I asked, 'About what?' He said, 'About anything you feel like talking about.' In the 'old days' they would have happily given me poison. My position has remained unchanged. Any attempt to give a racial/racist definition of an Afrikaner can count me out. Suddenly this point of view does not seem to be as outlandish as previously thought.

One of my more extraordinary experiences in this regard was when I was invited to open a conference in Orania. The founder of Orania is Prof. Carel Boshoff. I first met him 47 years ago. I had just written my final school examinations, and with a group of mates we went for a five-day hike over the mountains and through the streams of what was then the Eastern Transvaal. On the fifth day we ended up near Trichardtdal at a mission station of the

Dutch Reformed Church. Out of a very humble little cottage walked a man who introduced himself as Carel Boshoff. He also happened to be the son-in-law of Hendrik Frensch Verwoerd, the architect of apartheid. Over the years we have had many public debates. Although we have differed fundamentally, our relationship has always been one of mutual respect.

When he asked me to open the conference, I said to him, 'You know what my position is.' He said, 'Yes.' I said, 'Can Jakes Gerwel or Neville Alexander [both political activists and classified Coloured by the previous Government] come and live in Orania if they wanted to?' He said, 'Let my son answer that.' Young Carel said, 'Yes.' I said, 'In that case, I will come.' As it happened, Jakes Gerwel was also invited to speak at the conference. The theme was 'Community and Self-Sustainability'.

Orania is approximately one-and-a-half hours' drive from Kimberley airport towards Hopetown and on the banks of the Orange River. It has about six hundred inhabitants, all Afrikaans-speaking and all 'White'. I was driven around and shown how it managed to maintain itself agriculturally, educationally and economically. It even has its own currency, the 'Ora'. That evening, when introducing me, Oom Carel said, 'When I saw this man 47 years ago, I said to myself – This is a Boerseun, an Afrikaner.' In responding I said to him that I thought I knew what he was trying to say, but that my position remains the same. I told the audience that on the flight from Johannesburg to Kimberley I sat next to a Black man who was on the city council of Kimberley and whose home language is Afrikaans. I said, 'Oom Carel, that man is as much part of my language community as you are.' Well, I am still here to write about it.

Stripped of all its ideological baggage, Orania is a model of self-sustaining rural development. If there could be a dozen Orania-type settlements in the North-West and Eastern Cape, they would make a serious dent in rural poverty in South Africa.

For most of my intelligent life I have been aware of being stereotyped as an Afrikaner. There is not much I could, or can, do about it. As Jean-Paul Sartre once said, 'You are a Jew because I look at you.' Even if I have offended all the stereotypes of what an Afrikaner is, I remain 'a wayward, rebel, atypical Afrikaner'. So be it. Others will have to make peace with me. I am at peace. At the same time I feel very strongly about maintaining and promoting Afrikaans as a spoken language. For this I make no apologies. Someone who has written extensively and comprehensively about problems of identity and being 'an Afrikaner' is Hermann Giliomee. Read especially his work *The Afrikaners*.

Conclusion

I have written about being a backroom factotum and facilitator in order to make a very simple point. I have been fortunate in being involved in a wide range of situations in the 'old' and the 'new' South Africa. From this I have learned a great deal; enough at least to be fairly confident that my observations about South Africa are not the product of invention or thumb-sucking.

CHAPTER 4

PHILANTHROPIC
RECONSTRUCTION

The year 1993 was an extraordinary one for South Africa.
Chris Hani was assassinated; Treurnicht and Tambo died;
Mangosuthu Buthelezi formed a 'Freedom Alliance' with
right-wing Afrikaner parties to oppose the trend of negotiations between the ANC and the NP; Mandela and De
Klerk jointly won the Nobel Peace Prize; Jacqui Mofo-
keng became the first Black Miss South Africa and was
pipped at the post for Miss World; Winnie Mandela's
sentence was reduced on appeal, and she was elected
president of the ANC's Women's League; some MK
members joined the NP; the Broederbond became non-
racial but remained gender-exclusive; twenty top trade-
union leaders wanted to become MPs in the new parliament; Mandela edited an edition of *Vogue* magazine; the
Conservative Party demanded the whole of the Orange
Free State as part of an 'Afrikaner Volkstaat', and the
Interim Constitution made provision for nine regional
prime ministers in the 'new South Africa'; Ronnie Kasrils,
Carl Niehaus and Helen Suzman each wrote a book; and
Breyten Breytenbach exhibited his paintings for the first
time in South Africa.

Of course, that is not all that happened. Early in the

year, one evening, out of the blue, George Soros called me from New York. The last time I had had any serious lengthy discussion with him was about seven years earlier when I was fundraising with Alex Boraine for the Dakar Conference. Like yesterday, I remember him opening the door of his 5th Avenue apartment in Manhattan, saying, 'Come in, I'm George Soros.' We seriously did not know anything about him, and had been set up to meet him by John Gershwin of the National Endowment for Democracy in Washington. Soros started talking about his philanthropic interests, and the words 'open society' kept cropping up. Eventually I asked him, 'Have you read the works of Karl Popper?' (In retrospect that was one of the most foolish questions I ever asked.) Not only had he read Popper, but had studied under him at the LSE, and when he made a lot of money, set up the Karl Popper Foundation in Switzerland which oversaw the funding of Open Society Foundations and networks scattered all over the world. Even when he explained this to us, it did not really sink in. Alex and I were more interested in raising funds for IDASA's Dakar Conference. We explained to Soros what we had in mind, and he said, 'I think under PW Botha your country is finished, but this meeting seems like a good idea. How much are you looking for?' He covered half the costs of the Dakar Conference.

Over the phone, after seven years during which I sent him all the audited accounts of the conference and also briefly asked him for US$50 000 to launch the Goree Institute, he said, 'I would like to start up an Open Society Foundation for South Africa (OSFSA). Would you be available to be chairman?' I said yes, but reminded him that he thought South Africa was finished. He laughed and said, 'Things are looking quite interesting now.' Because I accepted Soros's offer I had to resign from the board of IDASA as it could have led to a conflict of interest. I am happy to say that IDASA has flourished as an independent NGO throughout the transition, and does invaluable work in tracking and researching democratic consolidation and development in the 'new South Africa'.

He arrived in South Africa early in April 1993, and a period of intense discussions and packed appointments began before OSFSA was formally launched. Ironically, most who came to the launch wanted to hear from Soros how to become a billionaire, whereas he was more interested in discussing the concept of an Open Society. The first board of OSFSA consisted of Michael Savage, Executive Director (seconded from UCT where he was Acting Vice Chancellor); Alex Boraine, Executive Director of IDASA; Peter Sullivan, editor of *The Star*; Tony Heard, former editor of the *Cape Times* and then freelance journalist; Mamphela Ramphele, Deputy Vice Chancellor of UCT; Rhoda Kadalie, anthropologist at UWC; Advocate Fikile Bam; Khehla Shubane, researcher at CPS; Helen Zille, then Public Affairs Director at UCT; and GT Ferreira, businessman. I was chairman. (When I introduced Soros to Bishop Tutu, Tutu complained that the OSFSA leadership was 'too White', and he was looking straight at me when he said it.)

Soros started OSFSA with a budget of R45 million, and told us it was 'our money' to spend and if we did so wisely there would be more to come. For him to spend wisely was to pursue the ideals of an Open Society. The whole board was invited on a trip to Berlin, Budapest, Warsaw and Kiev from 1–12 October 1993 to familiarise ourselves with projects he supported in those countries. Thus we could learn how to pursue the ideals of an Open Society in South Africa. What struck me forcibly on that trip was how Soros personally involved himself with his projects, whether it was promoting an independent media; changing the legal system in conformity with the rule of law; training new civil servants; transforming education; or simply teaching business practice to people who had no concept of a market system. This was particularly the case in Ukraine. I remember talking to a group of young students in Kiev who had no idea of a business contract, or collateral. As one said, 'Here if you wanted to divorce, you had to phone Moscow.'

We listened to Soros when he opened the academic year for the Central-East European University in Budapest (which he started) and pledged an additional $100 million. What struck me was that in Soros's philanthropy, there was no immediate or obvious kickback for him as a businessman. In Eastern Europe he was certainly not buying influence or patronage to help him in his investments. If one argues that in the 'final analysis' there was some gratification for what he was doing with his project funding, one is drawn back to philosophical abstractions such as an 'open society' to make sense of his involvement.

While I was chairperson, OSFSA started off by giving R3 million to the Women's Development Bank, R1,5 million to the National Youth Development Forum, and similar amounts to promote schools of government, rural development, radio and education. Initially Soros was impatient at our slow rate of spending. I had to assure him that it was not a question of reluctance, but more a question of 'looking before we leap'. South Africa, for a long time, had been NGO country where huge amounts of aid money disappeared without trace and to no demonstrable effect. I was determined that OSFSA should not strengthen a rampant culture of entitlement that would undermine the very goals we hoped to promote.

In 1996 Soros asked me to help him broaden his Open Society initiative in southern Africa. I pointed out to him that I would have to relinquish my position as chair of OSFSA (also an unpaid position) in order to help him with his new initiative. As I retired from OSFSA, so did Michael Savage as executive director. The board was broadened to include people like Majunka Gumbi, Leah Qubashe, and Brigalia Bam as the new chair in my place. I am not quite sure exactly what happened, but Soros and Aryeh Neier, his chief executive of Open Society New York, were not impressed with the new board's attempts to find a successor for Michael Savage. Consequently Soros disbanded the existing board and founded a new board; Zora Dawood was appointed Savage's successor, and Azar Cachalia became the new chair. Gumbi, Qubashe, Kadalie and Bam were not reappointed.

Setting up a regional board is more easily said than done. Soros decided on nine SADC countries: Malawi, Zambia, Zimbabwe, Namibia, Mozambique, Angola, Botswana, Lesotho and Swaziland. Initially the idea was to create an Open Society Foundation in each country, but it soon became clear that this would be too cumbersome and clumsy. Open Society Initiative for Southern Africa (OSISA) was launched in 1997. I was the chair, and we had a board member from each one of the countries. How were they identified? With the extraordinary services of Kim Brice, my first executive director, a process of auditing NGOs in each country began. Soon one could weed out the *per diem* vultures and entrepreneurs, and identify the 'good ones', i.e. NGO leaders who delivered and were dedicated. From a final list, a representative was invited to join the main OSISA board. The new challenge was to create an Open Society Charter for the nine countries, keeping in mind that they differed in size, level of urbanisation, quality of government and legal systems, as well as economic resources and level of development. For each country three or four priority areas had to be identified, e.g. Angola – strengthening civil society, law and education; Malawi – AIDS and education; Swaziland – education, law and AIDS; etc. Common regional initiatives were identified, such as media, democracy-building, education. Each board member would in his/her way make it known that OSISA was open for business, i.e. that donor funding was available for projects. Project proposals were sent to the OSISA headquarters in Braamfontein, Johannesburg. These had to be evaluated in order to make grant money available. This in itself was, and remains, a mammoth task. Consequently programme officers for each project area were appointed, who had to sift through the requests, make recommendations to the board, and then monitor progress of each grant for a project and report back to the board. If the money was not properly applied in terms of the original requests, funding stopped immediately. The first progress evaluation was usually after about six months. OSISA works with a budget of ± $15 million per annum, and at each board meeting (about four times a year) approximately $2 million is allocated to projects. Lucy Mayoeto from Zambia took over from Kim Brice in 1999 until 2002, and was succeeded by Tawanda Muthasa from Zimbabwe. All three are exceptional executive officers, and OSISA is regarded as one of the shining stars in the OSI firmament.

I have dwelt on the creation of OSISA to drive home a few critical points on donors and aid. In the NGO world, one can distinguish between a donor NGO, a project NGO, and a facilitating NGO. A donor NGO gives away money; a project NGO pursues a particular project – AIDS, media, law, etc.; and a facilitating NGO holds workshops and conferences between NGOs with common project goals.

OSISA as a donor agency is a microcosm of OSI (Open Society Institute of New York, the overarching body over all other Open Society initiatives), and in a sense OSI is a microcosm of the G8, or World Bank, or UN Aid Agency. The central question is: 'How does one get a bang for your buck?' Through OSISA I know firsthand that it can be done, but then one needs a competent agent, i.e. a board, with competent executives and programme officers who can see that the money gets to the intended beneficiaries, and *most important of all* that the money is competently spent in pursuing the project for which aid was requested in the first place. So far the AU, NEPAD, Ecowas, SADC, etc. are more like *per diem* watering holes than competent agencies.

I resigned from the position of chair of OSISA in 2003, and Dr Reginald Matcheva Hove of Zimbabwe took over for two years, and is now succeeded by Musa Thlope from Swaziland – both excellent. Since then (2004) I have been appointed to the main board of OSI, which meets a few times a year to discuss funding across the whole range of Open Society Institute activities. From my involvement at that level I have more than enough reason to take great pride in the work of OSISA.

When I was still involved with OSFSA, Soros called me one day and said that if I could think of an initiative that could have an impact and fell outside the budget of OSFSA he was willing to consider it. I immediately thought of housing, and thus a group of four of us spent a weekend at Soros's Long Island home talking about an appropriate mechanism to stimulate housing development in South Africa. Thus NURCHA (National Urban Reconstruction Housing Agency) was born. Cedric de Beer was its CEO from the start, and has done a magnificent job. Initially the focus was on end-user finance (i.e. loans), helping emerging contractors (i.e. Black builders), and resolving community conflict in the area of provision of housing. NURCHA was launched in 1995, and by 2000 had assisted in building approximately 160 000 houses, and helping about seventy contractors to become independent. NURCHA's focus has shifted more to banking and loans, but it is unquestionably one of the flagships of successful project funding of OSI. By 2005 Soros had spent approximately R3 billion on projects in southern Africa since I became involved in the original establishment of OSFSA in 1993; and he is still supporting all the initiatives I have discussed. In June 2005 I sat in on the main board of OSI in Budapest and personally witnessed the distribution of about half a billion US dollars to Open Society initiatives all over the world.

Soros, as a person, does not evoke a neutral or dispassionate response. He is revered or rejected; loathed or liked; praised or insulted. In the 18 years I have known him I know that a lot of conclusions about him are based on inadequate understanding, or inadequate information. Soros would be the first to announce that he is not a saint. I have never helped him to make one cent, nor received any such in payment for services rendered. So, in saying what I think of him, I do not owe or depend on him for a living. I have, however, in a modest way, helped him to spend his money in philanthropic causes.

I have also come to know him personally and very informally. Without pushing my luck, I think I can call him a friend. He is a complex person but with an instinctive sense for spotting a phony. And he hates being taken for a ride. At the same time, he can be instantaneously generous in supporting a cause which he believes has merit. The New York-based philanthropic structure that he has set up, OSI (Open Society Institute), is run by a very competent and dispassionate individual who started up Human Rights Watch, Aryeh Neier. Soros is guided by OSI's recommendations, but will sometimes strike out on his own, as he did with NURCHA.

He is not afraid to confront governments, but is also willing to work with them if he thinks they can promote the ideals of an Open Society. However, he will not just give money away because it gives him 'a warm feeling', no matter who is involved. I remember Mandela calling me to come and see him one evening. When I got to his house I found Helen Suzman, Irene and Clive Menell, and the current representative of the Ford Foundation there as well. Mandela, who was still president at the time, came in and said that he happened to be the chancellor of the University of the North, and a number of students were in debt and not able to pay their study fees. He needed R1 million, and very quickly. The others present suddenly found a lot of objects occupying their interest, and Mandela looked straight at me. I said I would see what I could do. I phoned Aryeh Neier and asked him whether he would like to meet Mandela. He said he would be delighted. I said it would cost him R1 million. He said, 'No problem.' Two weeks later Neier handed him the cheque in Johannesburg, and Mandela gave me a copy of his book, *A Long Walk to Freedom*, which he signed, and called me a 'role model' for South Africans.

About a year later Mandela called me again, and this time he said he needed money for his African Peace Initiative. I pointed out to him that he would have to be slightly more specific otherwise Soros would not respond. He asked me to try in any case. When I contacted Soros, his reply was: 'I do not sign blank cheques.' I was in a difficult spot, but went to Mandela and as gently as possible suggested he gave content to his request, e.g. the travel, accommodation and salaries for two or three top executives, because Soros said he does not sign blank cheques. I recall the smile freezing on Mandela's face, and his eyes going hard. That was the last time he talked to me about raising money. In fact, it was the last time he talked to me one on one in a personal friendly manner.

I introduced Soros to Thabo Mbeki when Mbeki was already deputy president. It must have been around 1994-95. Soros was very keen to start with an internet library between South African universities, and Mbeki responded with enthusiasm. Later Mbeki, then president, appointed Soros to his International Advisory Council. As far as I know, Soros has not attended a meeting and was not quite sure how effective it was. Soros had in the mean time assisted with some civil society work in Zimbabwe, either through OSISA or personally. He became increasingly concerned at the deteriorating situation. In December 2003 I arranged for Soros and Neier to meet two of Morgan Tsvangerai's representatives in Johannesburg. They were Gift Machikinere and Roy Bennet, who was subsequently jailed by the Zimbabwean parliament for shoving minister Chinamasa to the floor when he taunted Bennet about the loss of his farms. The MDC representatives made it quite clear to Soros that no talks or negotiations were taking place between the MDC and Zanu (PF), i.e. the Zimbabwean government. Five days later, on 11 December, Soros met Mbeki in his office in the Union Buildings. Present were Soros, Stewart Paperin, Mbeki, Trevor Manuel and me. When it came to the issue of Zimbabwe, Mbeki said: 'Negotiations are far advanced. Only one or two clauses are outstanding,' and that he was on top of the situation. Afterwards, Soros said, 'I don't think he was lying to us. He must be fed information by someone who has infiltrated MDC and tells Mbeki what he wants to hear.' The way Trevor Manuel kept looking at the ceiling as Mbeki spoke made me feel Soros was overly generous in his assessment of the situation. (The MDC did subsequently find someone who they suspected was a mole.) After the June 2005 OSI meeting in Budapest, Soros wrote a strong condemnatory letter to Mbeki about his Zimbabwean policy. Whether Mbeki ever received it is another question. Too often letters of this kind float around the warren of gatekeepers with which Mbeki surrounds himself.

The first time I met Soros in New York in 1987, most of his philanthropy focused on the Soviet Union and Eastern Europe, and he was regarded as a menace by the leadership in most of those countries. I remember him saying then (1987), 'The Soviet Union is finished. I doubt whether it will see 1990 intact.' Gorbachev started with *glasnost* and *perestroika*, East European countries began asserting their drive for independence, and on 9 November 1989 the Berlin Wall came down. From then on 'organised communism' disintegrated.

Far from withdrawing, Soros became even more involved. In his native Hungary he founded the Central East European University in Budapest; and became involved in most of the former Soviet states, especially Georgia and Ukraine but also Russia. Again the driving motive was to assist them in moving from closed to more open societies. He met Yeltsin, but according to those present, Yeltsin was too drunk to be coherent – it was 11 o'clock in the morning.

Soros then wrote an article in the *New York Review* which I quite frankly found astounding. In it he mentioned that he had met one of the new oligarchs, named

Bereshovsky, who told Soros that he had personally bankrolled Putin to succeed Yeltsin, and that Putin planted some bombs in Moscow which were used as a pretext to invade Chechnya and start a patriotic war, thus making sure of his succession to Yeltsin. I spoke to Neier and asked him if Soros had lost the plot. He said, 'No, it is true what George has said, but I am not sure it was wise to say it.' A few months later, after Bereshovsky and Putin had fallen out, Bereshovsky fled to London (with all his money), and on a BBC interview confirmed everything that Soros had written in the *New York Review*.

At the OSI meeting in June 2005 in Budapest, Soros singled out Putin and Bush as the greatest threats to liberal values and the ideal of an open society in the world. What made them so dangerous is that they did not change democratic constitutions, they simply co-opted their key supporting institutions, e.g. the Supreme Court, Parliament, civil service etc. At the latest meeting of OSI in Budapest (August 2005), a common report-back theme was that Soros was responsible for the 'colour revolutions', e.g. Ukraine and Georgia, and was destabilising Russia, China, etc. The whole issue of 'foreign-funded NGOs' has become a regime topic in many countries with authoritarian tendencies. Even President Mbeki has cleared his throat on this issue as far as South Africa is concerned. One wonders how South Africa's 'liberators' would have fared without foreign-funded NGOs.

A common stereotype about Soros is that he is a rich man who wants 'to do good'; that he has delusions of grandeur about changing states and societies. Nothing could be further from the truth. Soros does believe that societies, communities and individuals can improve, and that there are resources available to assist them to do so. But they can also abuse those resources, and it is important to recognise when they do so. Through my association with George Soros over the last 18 years, I have learned that philanthropy can be constructive and self-correcting. I am still learning a great deal from this association.

The name Karl Popper keeps cropping up in discussions about Soros, almost as if Soros is some uncritical devotee to a philosophical given. This is completely off the mark. The distinctive feature of Popper's philosophy is the fallibility of human knowledge; its progress through recognising mistakes; and a deep suspicion, even revulsion, for large-scale social engineering. Popper has certainly created more critical students than uncritical devotees. One such is Ernst Gellner who once said of Popper that '*The Open Societies and its Enemies* [Popper's famous two-volume exposition of his own philosophy] was written by one of the greatest enemies of the Open Society.' What makes Soros special is that as a philanthropist he has adopted the same self-critical style that Popper, Gellner and others have propagated.

CHAPTER 5

AN APPRENTICE
BUSINESSMAN

In the year 2005 I was non-executive chairman of Caxton
(Pty) Limited, and Adcorp Holdings (Pty) Limited. For a
brief period I was also non-executive chairman of Metro
Cash and Carry (Pty) Limited. I was also on the board as
non-executive director of First Rand. How I got to these
positions tells of my career as an apprentice to becoming
involved in the business world.

The Wits Business School offered me a position as visiting professor from 1990. It was convenient for us to
move to Johannesburg, because of our interests in Swaziland and because my wife Jane's parents were still alive. In
the mean time I had started a political consultancy called
Strategic Foresight, and Wits Business School wanted me
to teach a course on the political environment of business.

Some time in 1991 a young stockbroker in Johannesburg came to see me about how Black South Africans
could become more involved in corporate economic life
in South Africa. His name is Jurgen Kögl, a German
Namibian with enormous intellectual and physical energy
and a great enthusiasm for life. He and some of his colleagues wanted me to put them in touch with some leadership figures in the ANC, as well as professional Black

people in general, as they had a proposal to make which they believed could facilitate Black involvement in corporate South Africa. The idea was to create an investment trust called Khula (Zulu for 'growth') which would be Black-owned and would buy up viable medium-to-small-sized companies and use White experience to transfer managerial skills. A series of meetings were arranged in which people like Thabo Mbeki, Don Mkhwanazi, Mzi Khumalo, Nthato Motlana, Oscar Dhlomo, Sam Motsuenyane, Jurgen and I participated. It was decided to launch Khula Investment Trust (KIT) only after we had some financial commitments from some of the major business enterprises in South Africa. The idea was to borrow the money and repay at prevailing interest rates as the businesses that KIT bought prospered. So with people like Mzi Khumalo and Don Mkhwanazi I visited various well-known private-sector companies and explained the concept. They feigned, in the main, great excitement, even enthusiasm for the idea, but nobody grabbed for a cheque book. Eventually the Khula concept died on the vine through lack of corporate involvement.

Kögl and I then decided to form our own profit-making investment and consultancy company, and call it Khula in any case. We invited Mzi Khumalo, Max Maisela and Khehla Shubane to become equal partners, with Enos Mabuza and Zanele Mbeki from the Women's Development Bank (WDB) to serve on the board as advisors. Khula Investment Trust was one of the first Black majority-owned business companies in the 'new South Africa', if not the very first.

Before KIT was formed, early to mid-1992, Doug Band, CEO of Argus Holdings, asked if I would attend a very confidential meeting at the house of Pat Retief who was the CEO of JCI. Both gentlemen represented a substantial slice of 'English press' ownership in South Africa. (I wish to stress that the 'press barons' approached me, not I them.) The purpose of the meeting was to explore the possibility of creating an Independent Media Trust (IMT) into which Argus newspapers would be sold. The board of this Trust would have to have 'substantial' Black membership, but had to remain 'politically non-aligned'. Part of the motivation for such a Trust was a concern for the continued 'independence of the press' in the 'new South Africa'.

Another part of the motivation was to deal with the view, particularly among the majority of the people in South Africa, that the 'English press' was owned, controlled and manipulated by the 'mining houses' or 'big capital'. I remember HF Oppenheimer complaining to George Soros at a dinner in Brenthurst that 'We have all the disadvantages and none of the advantages of ownership.' For some time the 'mining houses' had been flailing about, trying to find themselves a formula to rid themselves of this political albatross, without, as it were, throwing the baby out with the bath water. It soon became clear that the meeting at Retief's home was another such attempt. It was generally agreed that the principle of the IMT was a good one (there were some broad hints that I could be its first chairman), and that we would meet again to report progress. In the mean time, Doug Band would keep in touch with me. He and Michael Spicer of Anglo American met with me a few times, and it was always 'Mutter, mutter, IMT important, you chairman, mutter,

mutter,' and so on. Nothing happened for a couple of weeks.

In the mean time, some representatives of the 'alternative press', including Guy Berger, then editor of *South*, came to see me. The 'alternative press' consisted of newspapers that fell outside the ownership and support of the big newspaper groups, whether Afrikaans or English, and were virtually completely donor-dependent. Most of their funds came from outside agencies such as foreign governments and foundations. That is why they could afford to be 'alternative', i.e. more independent and critical of the establishment than newspapers that depended on either political patronage and/or 'the market'. Now that 'the struggle' was over, funds were drying up, and many of these newspapers faced a survival crisis. Having been on the board of *Die Suid-Afrikaan* and *Vrye Weekblad*, and having been involved with fundraising for both, I knew exactly the nature of the dilemma. The representatives of the 'alternative press' were thinking of forming an 'Independent Media Diversity Trust' (IMDT – take out the 'D' and you have IMT), with the hope of getting generous parting donations from foreign donors that would help the Trust to assist smaller non-establishment newspapers. If the IMDT were to be formed, would I consider being its chairman? I said I was somewhat confused, and would first have to consider what had become of the IMT initiative.

This mystery was solved when a few days later Doug Band told me that the IMT plan could not get off the ground because, inter alia, they could not structure the shareholding in such a way as to prevent a 'hostile takeover' (i.e. politically aligned, i.e. ANC). However, he said: 'A far less ambitious but worthy cause was to set up a Trust to support "alternative newspapers".' The IMDT was duly launched in the latter part of 1992. It died on the vine through lack of foreign funding and absolutely pathetic support from the likes of the Argus Group, Nasionale Pers, etc. Virtually all the newspapers of the 'alternative press' have disappeared. Some of them, e.g. *Vrye Weekblad*, *South*, *New Nation* and *Die Suid-Afrikaan*, played a valuable role in 'the struggle'.

However, the launch of the IMDT did not address the problem that motivated the creation of the IMT at the meeting at Pat Retief's home, namely the ownership of the 'English press' in South Africa. By the time Khula was formed in early 1993, and owing to me being drawn into the newspaper world by the 'press barons' and the IMDT, I had got pretty fired up about the importance and dilemma of the 'English press' and its independence in a 'new South Africa'. I realised that the Argus Group, for example, was 'in play', and Kögl and I, with great enthusiasm, no experience and no money, started stalking the Argus Group. That is how I got involved with Terry Moolman and Noel Coburn of Caxton (Pty) Limited. Moolman proposed that we joined forces and made a bid for the Argus Group. I arranged meetings with Julian Ogilvie Thompson, Spicer, Band and Vaughan Bray for Moolman and me. Each time we were received with polite smiles bordering on contempt. I even had a lunch with Mr HF Oppenheimer at the Ritz in Paris to discuss the purchase of the Argus Group. His response was vague and he suggested I talk to JOT (Julian Ogilvie Thompson).

The point is they all knew exactly what was going on and we were simply being tolerated and humoured. They had had dealings with Tony O'Reilly, President of Heinz Inc., and while we (Moolman, Coburn, Kögl and Slabbert) thought we were in with a chance, they had already decided to sell 31% interest in Argus newspapers to O'Reilly's Independent Group. Band, O'Reilly and JOT featured on the front page of *The Star* under the heading 'A Deal Between Like-minded Gentlemen'. We certainly were not in that league. I wrote a rather impassioned letter to Band telling him how I had felt abused and manipulated. He and Spicer came and personally apologised. I should have become accustomed to the ruthless 'bottom line' thinking of business when it comes to matters political and social. Virtually the whole business establishment had abandoned me during the Tricameral Referendum in 1983 for 'a step in the right direction'. When Tony Bloom, then CEO of Premier Milling, took me to ask Sol Kerzner for funds for the PFP, Kerzner sat playing with his worry beads surrounded by his flunkies and said, 'Why must I give money away to a party that talks to f... communists?' I got up and left, and Tony rushed after me, saying: 'Don't you want to ask him?' I said, 'I would not ask him for five cents to go to a railway toilet.' By then Kerzner had allegedly bribed virtually any 'homeland leader' where he wanted casino rights. These were 'the collaborators' who the ANC demanded should be killed and 'their heads crushed like snakes'. (On 18 June 1992 Sol Kerzner picked up the bill for Thabo's 50th birthday bash in Sun City, attended by Joe Slovo and, of course, Thabo.) As a matter of fact, Stella Sigcau, who is

132

on Mbeki's cabinet, also collaborated with Kerzner when she headed up the Transkei homeland, and when Bantu Holomisa exposed her corruption he was promptly expelled from the ANC.

I met O'Reilly at Oxford when I addressed the Oxford Union in a debate in 1985. His son was then running for president of the Oxford Union. We got on well together, and still do. However, when I went to see him in 1986 on the 91st floor of the Heinz Building in Pittsburgh to raise funds for the Dakar Conference, he said to me, 'Look, you're a hell'uva nice guy, and I like you, but I do not fund projects that involve communists.' (At that time he was pretty close to Mugabe because of Heinz's interests in Zimbabwe. Mugabe was a Maoist – does that not make him a communist?) Later on he gave Mandela a hundred thousand dollars and has visited his game lodge near Welgevonden. Welgevonden is a 'high-class' game lodge in the Warmbaths area. Douw Steyn built himself a lavish game lodge next to it, and, it is rumoured, one for Mandela as well.

Talking of Mandela's game lodge: Douw Steyn of Auto and General built a house for himself in Johannesburg which subsequently was launched as the Saxon Hotel. Dick Enthoven told me that Douw Steyn would like to meet me. It was about the beginning of 1992. I met him in his enormous house, sitting all alone. He said: 'Van Zyl, this house is yours to use as you see fit: meetings, workshops, accommodation, etc. All I ask in return is that you introduce me to this "new lot".' I invited him to a meeting at Jesus College, Cambridge, between South Africans and residents of the UK. There Douw Steyn met Thabo Mbeki and

133

some other ANC heavies. That was the last time I had any serious dealings with Douw Steyn. The next I heard was that Mandela had left Winnie and moved into Douw's house. He was pampered and looked after for quite a while, and of course moved out when he became president. At the launch of the Saxon, Mandela made the speech and his opening line was: 'It is because of businessmen like Douw Steyn that apartheid came to its knees.' I quietly left. Enough said.

In 2004 I was sitting next to O'Reilly's wife at a dinner party, and in small talk asked her what they were doing and when they were leaving. She said, 'We are spending the weekend at Mandela's game lodge. You know, the one Douw Steyn built him, next to Welgevonden. And then we go home.' As I said, I am only an apprentice businessman.

Because of our joint experience in stalking the Argus Group, Moolman asked Kögl and me, in our capacity as members of Khula, to help Caxton win the tender for printing the telephone directories. We involved WDB and were successful; Caxton got the contract. Moolman was so grateful that he bankrolled Khula into buying 15% stake in Adcorp Holdings. At that time the share was trading at 90 cents. Adcorp must have been the first listed company that sold 15% of its interests to a majority Black-owned company, for that is what Khula (Pty) Limited was at that time. It was very short-lived, however. John Barry, CEO of Adcorp at the time, went on a very successful acquisition spree, and the share price traded at R33 at one stage. The Black partners of Khula, Mzi Khumalo, Khehla Shubane and Max Maisela, promptly sold their shares and bailed out. Overnight Khula was no longer Black majority-owned, and Adcorp no longer had genuine Black empowerment partners. KIT and Khula Consultancy formally came to an end at the end of 2003; although I have no business or financial connections with Jurgen Kögl, we are still friends.

In the mean time I was approached by both Adcorp and Caxton to become non-executive chairman, a position I occupy at the time of writing (August 2005). Although I am formally non-executive, I have become very much involved in the working of both companies, and have learned a great deal. I have learned, particularly from Terry Moolman of Caxton and Richard Pike, CEO of Adcorp, that it is possible to do honest business. It is not always very easy, and it does not necessarily make one very popular, but it can be done. By honest business, I mean not buying political favours, paying bribes or sacrificing your independence. It also means not dabbling in so-called 'Black economic empowerment' (BEE) for show or being politically correct.

I have observed with fascination and sometimes bewilderment how the philosophy of BEE has evolved and penetrated South African corporate life. Initially it was as crude as Douw Steyn's request to introduce him to 'the new lot'. It was as simple as 'introduce me to a Black with some serious political connections and we can do business'. There are businessmen who had been quite content to bribe and do business with the apartheid government who were willing to do the same with 'the new lot' with equal enthusiasm. And, of course, there were available Black partners who were not backward in coming forward to pursue profits that were previously inaccessible to them. And why not? I do not begrudge Dr Motlana, Justice Dikgang Moseneke, Sakkie Macozoma or Cyril Ramaphosa one cent that they made out of NAIL, but I have severe doubts whether this is an appropriate model for pursuing and promoting Black Economic Empowerment. The same can be said of Mzi Khumalo's takeover of JCI Mining.

The first wave of Black 'enrichment' created a few unfortunate trends. First, if you are the 'right Black' at the right place and at the right time, you can become wealthy irrespective of competence or effort. Secondly, it unleashed a frenzy of conspicuous consumption – cars, houses, clothes, etc. First prize must go to Mzi Khumalo who hired Onassis's yacht for the Cannes Festival and the Olympic Games. One of the emerging Black corporate leaders who was a guest on the yacht told me breathlessly, 'Do you know, the bar stools were covered in whale foreskins.' When I suggested that the whole exercise was a bit over the top, he said 'Van, you have no idea what this means to a piccanin from Soweto!' Thirdly, and inevitably, it created a growing sense of relative deprivation between the 'haves' and the 'have nots'. This will have political consequences in the near future. Fourthly, it strengthened a growing culture of corruption. A survey done by Research Surveys in July 2005 showed that 86% of South Africans of all races believed that 'corruption has become a way of life in South Africa'. Corruption is simply another way of making money without earning it.

It was inevitable that some form of official intervention had to come. The first attempt was to draw a clear distinction between individual enrichment and 'genuine Black empowerment'. Thus targets were set as far as equity, board appointments, executive appointments, skills development and social responsibility were concerned. For a company to be 'genuinely empowered' it had to meet requirements in these different areas. Inevitably business life entered a period of 'shifting goalposts', 'fronting' and 'fast-tracking'. Almost immediately some difficulties presented themselves. For example, it was impossible to develop a 'one-size-fits-all' model to apply to companies that varied greatly in size, complexity and expertise. Secondly, who decides whether a company is properly empowered? And do the same set of rules for government tenders and private competition apply? Thirdly, the dilemma of the 'golden handcuff' immediately became apparent. If, for example, a company had to have 20-25% equity in 'Black' hands, what prevented Black shareholders from selling when the time was ripe? Should they only be allowed to sell to other Black shareholders in order to preserve the BEE status of the company? And where would the new shareholders get the money, etc. etc.? The latest attempt is to legislate a Broad Based Black Economic Empowerment Act. The underlying philosophy is that in various economic, industrial and business sectors, 'charters' would be constructed, e.g. a Mining Charter, Financial Services Charter, etc. Each charter would be monitored by 'agencies' who would score the BEE credentials of companies working under the various charters.

I went to a seminar arranged by GIBS (Gordon Institute of Business Science) in May 2005 at which a specialist from DTI (Department of Trade and Industry) explained the intentions of the Act. He quite cheerfully started by saying that BBBEE was an attempt 'to promote capitalism by non-capitalist means'. I listened with a growing sense of *déjà vu* and dismay. The only difference between apartheid law and BBBEE law was that, whereas the former tried to legislate racial entitlement for the minority, the latter wished to legislate racial entitlement for the majority. The apartheid policy had various key acts: Population Registration, Group Areas, Separate Amenities, Section 10 Urban Areas Consolidation Act, the Homeland Government Act, etc. Each act was in effect a 'charter', and under each act a whole special bureaucracy (agencies) were created to see to the implementation of the intention of the acts. Eventually the whole apartheid edifice collapsed under the weight of bureaucratic inefficiency and corruption. It is difficult to see the BBBEEA not going the same way. And it does not even have the guidelines of a Population Registration Act. At the risk of repetition, let me state the problem as clearly as I can. The BBBEEA states that 'Black people is a generic term which means Africans, Coloureds and Indians'. This, however, begs the question: in the old days race was defined by the Population Registration Act, a piece of legislative solipsistic nonsense. In the new BBBEEA there is no such legislative definition. It merely states who 'Black people' are without defining how to identify Coloured, Indian or African. There is now also an attempt to get Chinese in South Africa accepted as 'Black'. It is not difficult to anticipate what is going to happen. Just as under the old Population Registration Act a whole cohort of lawyers were spawned to advise customers how to circumvent the presumed intentions of the Act, so it will be the case with current attempts at BBBEE. Secondly, corruption is bound to flourish.

The point, of course, is that the whole empowerment initiative tries to address an extremely important and valid problem: how to make the majority effective participants in corporate South African life. This was exactly the problem that the initial attempt to create the Khula Investment Trust tried to address. But even then it was blindingly obvious that there were no easy short cuts. There had to be a transfer of competence and efficiency, capital had to be made available in a financially sound and accountable manner, and a culture of 'artificial entrepreneurship' had to be strongly guarded against. Those remain the challenges, and I am convinced they can be met. But then we must give up the 'one-size-fits-all' approach, even within so-called 'charters'. There are impressive attempts currently being pursued in business.

It is equally important not to confuse 'Black economic empowerment' (BEE) with the challenge of alleviating poverty and promoting socio-economic development. I do not for one moment think that a 'trickle down' effect from 'powerful economic growth' will do the trick. Some form of state intervention is necessary, especially in the areas of housing, health, education and service delivery. This also does not mean that business or the private sector have no role to play in these areas. Combating growing unemployment is a meeting point with a common focus for the public and private sectors.

In a special edition of the ANC's magazine *Umrabulo* (no. 23) under the heading 'Development and Underdevelopment', the ANC spokesmen show a clear and compelling understanding of this dilemma, so it is not my intention to show them how to suck eggs. However, it is one thing to have an excellent articulation of policy, but another to have effective implementation. The article displays a clear awareness of this dilemma as well. Major challenges are to develop the appropriate 'political will' and understanding amongst its own support base; to combat corruption fiercely and resolutely at all levels; and to persuade the beneficiaries of the 'first economy' (i.e. predominantly Whites) to assist in grappling with the problems experienced by those who are deprived in the 'second economy' (i.e. predominantly Blacks).

When I discuss issues of BBBEE I do so not at an analytical/philosophical level, but more from an experiential level, i.e. in my capacity as non-executive chairman of the listed companies Adcorp Ltd and Caxton Ltd. Both companies are listed on the JSE, and both have grappled seriously, and I believe honestly, with broadening Black economic empowerment efficiently. They differ in size (Caxton being much larger), complexity, and customer and client base. The assets of Adcorp are predominantly people, i.e. intellectual capital, and it focuses on staffing, communications and market research. Caxton is a printing, publishing, packaging and newspaper company. Although its assets are also people, enormous capital investment goes into machinery and equipment.

In both instances I have sat in on 'beauty parades', i.e. listening to prospective Black equity partners explaining why they should become part of the company. Arguments vary from blatant entitlement ('You owe it to us, it is now pay-back time') where they demand shares without indicating how they are going to be financed, or being 'decorative', i.e. where they can assess that the company is profitable, will continue to grow, are prepared to pay for the shares, but have no intention or idea how to add value to the performance of the company; to those that demonstrate a serious wish to add value, and grapple with the executives of each company on how best to achieve this. The 'race card' is flashed generously when potential partners are rejected. However, there has never been, in either company, nor will there be, an attempt to buy 'political correctness'.

The other levels of empowerment, e.g. board appointments, transferring skills and promoting management and executive personnel, present different challenges to the two companies. To insist on unrealistic targets or goals in order to score 'brownie points' for being a BEE company defeats the whole purpose of broadening empowerment in corporate economic life in South Africa. I am sufficiently optimistic that unimplementable policies eventually become redundant. I only hope not too much damage is done before that happens.

CHAPTER 6

TAKING STOCK

One can talk our country up, or one can talk it down. Both perspectives are not necessarily mutually exclusive: it is not all good, but then again, it is not all bad. It also depends at which level one pitches one's analyses: are we looking at the performance of government at the different levels; or the performance, or lack of it, in the formal or informal economy; or the various aspects of social life, e.g. health, education, law and order; or demography, e.g. urban vs. rural life, age, gender and distribution of the population; or at the scope and performance of civil society; or at political organisations and movements; or at diversity and the position of minorities, etc. etc.? Focusing on one or two levels to the exclusion of all the others can make one either simplistically pessimistic or optimistic about the future.

In general, I prefer to talk my country up. A key question I usually ask of any country is: How is stability maintained? If one puts the variable of stability on a continuum ranging from repression to consent, the next question would be: is stability largely the consequence of state repression, or voluntary consent on the part of the majority of citizens? In South Africa, despite the enormous challenges we face, we have predominantly consensual stability, i.e. the majority of citizens, interest groups and organisations, whatever their differences, buy into the existing order and the manner in which change should come about. The government does not rely on coercion to force conformity, and there are no serious threats from society itself violently to overthrow the status quo.

Why do we have consensual stability? In the first place because of the kind of constitution we adopted in 1996. It is a classic liberal democracy – the hallmark of such a democracy is *not* the celebration of majoritarianism, but the constraint it places on the abuse of power and tyranny. That is why such passionate debate is unleashed when parties and interest groups suspect government of co-opting or abusing the Constitution.

Secondly, the Constitution makes provision for supporting mechanisms, e.g. the Constitutional Court, to guarantee and protect human rights and civil liberties. Generally speaking, no law-abiding citizen feels that 'big brother' is watching you. On the contrary, individuals and interest groups can mobilise to protest or pursue their collective goals. The right to freedom of association, even the right for workers to strike, is guaranteed by the Constitution.

Thirdly, and flowing from the first two, we have an active and vibrant civil society. The term 'civil society' refers to that space between the state and the individual where voluntary organisations can be created to pursue collective goals that do not have to be controlled or regulated by the state, provided they do not offend the Constitution, from TAC (Treatment Action Campaign) to the

143

formation of sport clubs, women's organisations, youth leagues, trade unions, etc. Into this context falls a relatively free and independent media. Memories are short, but the older generation will recall how controlled and constrained public discourse was under the previous regime. I am constantly amazed at the critical engagement of columnists and presenters, and the degree of voluntary participation from citizens on radio and TV talk shows. It is very difficult, if not impossible, to find a holy cow. Think of commentators like Rhoda Kadalie, Barney Ntombothi, Mathata Tsedu, Xolela Mangcu and Sipho Seepe.

After more than ten years of consensual stability, most of us take its benefits for granted and even get quite irritated when someone reminds us how fortunate we are. Our response is almost: 'So what? That's the way it should be.' Those of us with longer memories know that for a hell of a long time, that's not the way it was.

Under conditions of repressive stability one measures the wellbeing of society by the performance of government. How repressive is it of human rights? Who does it persecute or oppress? How does it plunder the assets of society? Under conditions of consensual stability it would be a mistake to equate the wellbeing of society with the performance of a democratic government. Sometimes societies make steady and stable progress not because of but in spite of the performance of government. Democratic governments can sometimes behave so appallingly that the voters simply get rid of them by voting for another one.

All that one can hope for from a democratic government is that it develops the ability to recognise its mistakes sooner rather than later, and does not repeat them. What are the most common mistakes?

- Confusing democratic representivity with competence: The fact that you are the duly elected representative does not automatically give you the competence to make your promises come true. A local councillor does not automatically have the competence to reticulate water, allocate electricity or administer rates and taxes. And when he/she retrenches or fires the official who has such competence, you have a self-concocted crisis of delivery.
- Rewarding loyalty above competence: The leader appoints those who are compliant and uncritically support him/her because he/she values control more than performance. Thus manifestly incompetent cabinet ministers strut around pronouncing nonsense, and compound the problem by appointing officials who are of the same ilk.
- Confusing authority with intelligence: A very common mistake. I remember nice young Afrikaner boys who came to Parliament in 1974 and five or six years later became ministers or deputy ministers. Suddenly their whole demeanors changed. The back stiffened, the suits became more expensive, and they pronounced the words 'yes' and 'no' as if they were pregnant with profundity. They automatically assumed that because they had authority they must be clever.
- Dealing with corruption selectively: As leader you know that the cabinet minister sitting next to you has

145

his/her fingers in the till, but you deliberately divert attention from this person by jumping on a minor official selling fake IDs in Mpumalanga to show that you are serious about combating corruption. The rule is simple: the bigger the fish you catch, the more seriously you will be taken as an angler. Corruption is corruption is corruption.

- Sacrificing domestic policy for foreign policy: This is also a mistake of repressive governments, but as they are not accountable to anyone but themselves, it resonates far more strongly with democratic government. The absent leader syndrome very quickly translates into perceptions of indifference about domestic problems and crises.

All these mistakes were abundantly evident in the democratically elected government of the United States of America in the wake of the Katrina catastrophe. I could hardly suppress a smile when I read of Essop Pahad sermonising the US for their shortcomings in this regard. A quiet walk around in his own backyard could hopefully be a humbling experience. Why not start with a few squatter communities – Delmas, Steenberg or Knoppieslaagte, Protea South, etc.?

I have no intention of adding yet another psychoanalysis on the deep primordial urges that drive our president Thabo Mbeki. Seldom has a head of state had so many biographers writing about him at the same time, and nobody is quite sure who is authorised to do so. I got to know him as an extremely intelligent and analytically gifted individual; he is also a bit paranoid: 'Someone is always out to get him.' He has appointed some very competent members of cabinet only to detract from their competence by appointing some thundering dunderheads. The average voter is not quite sure how government works, or whether it works at all. This is compounded by the kind of electoral system we have adopted: closed–list proportional representation combined with floor–crossing. Like achieving the opposite of what you claim to pursue: being democratic in an undemocratic way. You pretend you vote for us, and we pretend we represent you.

Economists generally are quite bullish about the growth prospects of the South African economy. They always remind one that we came off a base of 1% in 1994 per annum growth, and now hover around 3,5% to 4%, with 6% seen as not completely unrealistic for the next ten years. This is no mean feat from a government that, during 'the struggle', promised 'festive socialism' and 'redistributive populism'.

But it is precisely those promises that are now coming back to haunt them. Indices to measure quality of life paint a depressing picture. The human development report released by UNDP (United Nations Development Plan) makes for sobering reading. It shows that in the last 11 years in South Africa, life expectancy has dropped, income inequality has increased, and levels of educational enrolment have declined dramatically. In short, the poorest of the poor have become more, and poorer.

I have no simple remedy to offer. Of course we need more foreign and domestic investment; of course we need to broaden the skills base; of course we have to combat corruption on all fronts at all levels, but who will do it, and how and when? Mbeki and his advisers have analysed and written far more extensively on these problems than I intend to. The simple question is – when do we move from defining the problem to attacking it?

The advantage of a repressive regime is that it can afford to ignore these problems. It simply disintegrates into a plundering state, stealing the remaining assets of the country and salting away the proceeds offshore. In this way, Dos Santos of Angola is reputed to be the second-wealthiest person in Brazil.

But for a democratically elected government, these problems translate into a massive crisis of delivery. This crisis becomes the interface between poor and well-off; between unemployed and employed; between squatter township and suburb; between unhoused and housed, etc. The only thing that straddles this divide is the vote. That is why the crisis of delivery holds the potential to become a crisis for democracy. If one places voter response on a continuum that ranges from apathy to activism, the question is: which side will predominate? Voter activism is not a bad thing democratically speaking. It means voters wish to engage the democratic structures to redress perceived wrongs. (This is the positive message from the so-called Zuma affair.) Apathy, on the other hand, must not be confused with inaction. Voter apathy says: 'A curse on all your houses, we will take the law into our own hands.' This can translate into vigilantism, plundering services such as water and electricity, and escalating crime and looting. And therein lies the crisis for democracy. Eventually the only way government can deal with this kind of activism is to use the instruments of repression, e.g. police and army. South Africa is not quite there yet, but in certain regions and communities things are looking ominous.

The well-off are largely oblivious of the crisis of delivery, and to a certain extent are even protected from it. I have no doubt that this crisis will become the most important issue influencing the succession of the current president at the ANC National Congress in 2007. As I understand it, the provincial congresses nominate the top six positions of the ANC executive: president, deputy president, secretary general, etc. These nominations are sent to the National Congress, and if there is unanimity these positions are automatically filled. Thus Thabo Mbeki became president, Zuma deputy, and so on. If there is no unanimity, the names are voted for from the floor of Congress. In addition to these positions, the National Executive Council is elected from the floor of Congress. Last time Trevor Manuel got the most votes, with Cyril Ramaphosa second, Winnie Mandela third, and so on.

President Mandela tried to set a precedent whereby the president of the ANC became the president of the country. Thabo Mbeki has now hinted that this need not necessarily be the case, i.e. that he could still be head of the ANC without being head of the country. This raises all kinds of dilemmas. Let us assume he is successful in becoming head of the ANC through the nine provincial congresses but does not serve as president of the country, because the Constitution does not allow a president to serve more than two terms. Mbeki has already indicated that he does not wish to change the Constitution, so the question arises: How will the president of the country be chosen if Mbeki is successful in remaining president of the

ANC for a third term? Consider two possibilities: the president of the country, like the NEC, is elected from the floor of Congress. Given the crisis of delivery it is unlikely that Mbeki has sufficient control over Congress to determine his favoured successor via this route. So you could end up with a president of the country who is hostile to the president of the ANC. The second possibility is that Mbeki's government enacts a bill in parliament which, like the old NP of apartheid years, says that the president of the country will be elected by the parliamentary caucus of the ruling party. Now this is a far more palatable route for Thabo Mbeki. Remember, as leader of the ANC and until 2009 president of the country, given a closed-list PR system, he can have a decisive influence on who becomes a member of Parliament. Given the current complacency of the ANC caucus it is far more likely that Thabo's 'man' or 'woman' will be his successor. All this presupposes that Zuma will still be embroiled in legal battles. If he is cleared, all bets are off, and I have no doubt that Zuma will exploit the crisis of delivery to the hilt. Already rumours are beginning to circulate that Mbeki has effectively lost control of the ANC outside parliament.

The region where I suspect the crisis of delivery is reaching acute proportions is the Cape Peninsula. This is for obvious demographic and socio-economic reasons. It was for a long time the so-called Coloured Labour Preference area under the NP government, and Blacks were prevented from coming to Cape Town. Of course, with the advent of the new South Africa, millions of Black South Africans poured into the Peninsula from the Transkei and Ciskei. It is, however, abundantly clear that the Peninsula is infrastructurally completely unable to cope with this influx. Apart from wine, fruit, fisheries and tourism, there is no significant economic base for expansion, and there is a massive over-supply of unemployable workers. Crime must increase as a route to physical survival. This government faces some difficult trade-offs. Does it focus on delivery of basic services to Black voters at the expense of Coloured voters? If so, it risks losing political control of the Western Cape. Signs of tension between these communities are increasing on almost a daily basis. An erstwhile struggle activist told me recently that 'this ANC government has made me feel more Coloured than I ever felt under the Nats.' And he is an ANC supporter. Watch this space in the run-up to the 2009 elections.

By the way, the situation in which the leader of the ruling party is not the president of the country is not without precedent. Currently, Namibia and Malawi are examples. Nujoma still leads SWAPO and so controls his president. Maybe Mbeki wishes to govern from such a political grave as well, who knows? There is, however, a major difference: South Africa is a much more complex, more urbanised country than any of its neighbours. In addition, the defence and police forces are not poised for a coup. South Africa is simply not a country that can be grabbed by the throat and shaken around like a rag doll. It is not given to any man or woman to unilaterally and uncontestedly impose his/her will on our country. Therein lies the excitement and fascination of our politics.

This does not prevent some analysts from looking at South Africa as if it is in the grip of some Marxist-Leninist

151

clique, and rubbishing the present and future of the country. Even if it is so that some intellects in government crave for a 'Gramscian hegemony' over the masses, they haven't got a snowball's hope in hell. The scope and diversity of civic action simply defies such hegemony. Voluntary associations in the areas of literacy, health, skills development, business management, orphan care, combating AIDS, perform magnificently. I have met and observed many of them. Of course, government can play an important enabling role, but if it does not do so, it will simply be regarded as irrelevant. There is a boundless arrogance in the notion that you have the right to tell ordinary common-sense folk how and what to think.

I have been extremely fortunate to have met and been befriended by some extraordinary common-sense folk. I think of MT Moerane, who in 1970 was editor of *The World*. We, together with Buthelezi, Curnick Ndamse, Pat Poovalingham, Colin Eglin and Japie Basson, formed in 1970 a discussion group called 'Synthesis'. The prime mover was actually a Cape medic called Lou van Oudenhove. We met monthly for open-ended discussions on 'the state of the nation'. After one such meeting I was driving MT to the airport over flyovers and four-laned highways, and with a quiet chuckle he said: 'You Whites are very good to us Blacks. You are building all these beautiful highways, so that when we take over we won't have to start from scratch.' From him I also learned first-hand of the depth of anger and frustration of the elite in Soweto. I was teaching at Stellenbosch in 1970-71, and belonged to another discussion group. Piet Koornhof came to address it, I think as deputy minister of Bantu administration. Apparently the government had commissioned research on 'the urban Bantu', and Koornhof came to give us a confidential briefing on the results. He painted an extraordinarily rosy picture, saying that 'basically the urban Bantu were quite happy, not interested in politics, and only wanted a job and a house'.

I suggested to my colleague and friend Jannie Gagiano that I contact MT Moerane and ask him to arrange a house meeting in Soweto so that Gagiano and I could pose as NP spokesmen and come and tell them what the research said about the 'urban Bantu'. MT duly arranged a house meeting in Dube, and with a straight face, in about twenty minutes, I told the gathering of about seventy people what Koornhof had told us. For approximately three hours the anger and hatred washed over us. Eventually MT told them that we were actually Afrikaner dissidents from Stellenbosch University. Initially there was incredulity, then laughter, then partying into the early hours of the morning.

Fast forward. In 2003 I went to the offices of READ, a promotion-of-literacy NGO. I saw a grey-haired man sitting in the waiting room. He got up when he saw me and said: 'I don't know if you remember that night in Soweto when you told us about Koornhof. I just wanted to tell you that you never realised how close you two were to being killed that night.' MT is long gone. A wonderful friend.

I first met Ernie Malgas when he was in the 'underground' in Port Elizabeth. I was already Leader of the Opposition in the House of Assembly, and Andrew Savage, the MP for Walmer, set up the meeting in some back room.

Also present was Stone Sisane, who later became MEC for education in the Eastern Cape government. Ernie had spent ten years on Robben Island, and when he came out was rearrested and severely tortured. He was telling me about this when Stone interrupted him, saying, 'We were in the cell next door and at one stage he was "crying like a baby".'

The next time I saw Ernie Malgas was at Marly le Roy in Paris in 1989, when IDASA had arranged a meeting on future ANC economic policy. At the reception that evening Ernie drew me aside and started telling me of a Robben Island experience. He said, 'You know, Van, I was a cook on Robben Island.' Steve Tshwete who was present said, 'No Ernie, you cannot tell that story.' Ernie said, 'Never mind, he will understand.' He continued, 'There was a warder who was extremely cruel to us prisoners. One day he went to the mainland, and I cooked his dog.' Steve could no longer contain himself; he said, 'You know, Van, it was the best meal I had all the time I was in Robben Island.' 'Yes,' said Ernie, 'but do you remember when he came back we helped him for two days to look for his dog.'

The next I heard of Ernie was a few years later when Stone told me that Ernie had had a stroke and was lying on the floor of a shack in New Brighton. I said, 'Good God, Stone, the ANC is now the government, can't they do something to help him?' Stone said he had tried everything but to no avail. The last time I saw Ernie Malgas was on TV when he was wheeled in, in a wheelchair, to a TRC meeting. Alex Boraine looked at him and asked, 'Mr Malgas, please tell us about yourself.' Ernie looked up at the platform party with a look of dumbfounded bewilderment on his face. Then he slowly lowered his head into his hands and started sobbing uncontrollably. Tutu wept openly as they wheeled him out. A few months later he died in New Brighton. What a waste.

And then there is Dolly Dube from Vosloorus; a nursing sister, who at the height of the ANC-Inkatha violence in the early 90s converted her own house into a maternity home. It is now a modernised maternity hospital, and since those bitter days she has delivered more than ten thousand babies! In fact, White pregnant mothers prefer to go to Dolly Dube rather than to any government hospital. A person of irrepressible optimism and cheerfulness.

I only remember him as Eric, because that is the way he introduced himself. I was attending a protest meeting of squatters in the KTC area on the Cape Flats in 1974 led by Bishop Patrick Matolengwe. We were protesting against the Prevention of Illegal Squatting Amendment Act which sought to evict, primarily, squatters from the newly formed Crossroads. Then there were about ten thousand of them. This was the first piece of legislation I opposed in Parliament.

Eric came to me after the meeting and asked if I would come to his shack with him. When I got there I noticed an award for ten years' loyal service from the Metal Box Company hanging on the wall. He told me that he had been in the single quarters in Guguletu, and his wife and three children were living in the Transkei. Suddenly she appeared on his doorstep with their three children and said she could not survive on the money he was sending them. He then moved to Crossroads and built a shack for them. As fortune would have it, she fell pregnant and produced triplets. According to the traditional custom, Eric went to the Transkei and married a nurse to come and look after the six children as well as his wife, who had been paralysed by the birth. Eric pulled away the kitchen curtain and I saw his wife lying on the floor. He asked her to show me she was paralysed. I protested that it was not necessary.

He then asked me to seek an interview with the relevant minister, explain the situation, and ask for permission to remain in the Cape. The relevant minister happened to be Dr Andries Treurnicht. When I explained Eric's dilemma, he expressed sympathy but said there was a solution. Eric had to move back to the single quarters in Guguletu. His wife should go to a nursing home, and his nurse should take the children back to the Transkei and look after them there. When I told Eric this, he said in a very quiet voice, 'They must kill us here; because in the Transkei we will surely die.'

That was the last time I saw him. There were numerous raids on Crossroads, shacks demolished, and the people put on the train and sent back to the Transkei. Most of them got off at Worcester and came back. They were chased around like human guinea fowl. When I left Parliament in 1986, old Crossroads had more than a million people; new Crossroads was filling up to compete, and the government had been forced to build Khayelitsha.

I remain firmly convinced that apartheid was destroyed primarily because ordinary folk like these I have mentioned refused to acquiesce in their own destruction. Despite breaking up squatter camps, forced removals and the ruthless implementation of the pass laws, they came to the cities in their millions and 'White South Africa' began to evaporate. Apartheid self-destructed because of a massive crisis of delivery. Those ordinary folk are still around, only there are many more of them. And no amount of historical invention, racial romanticising or ideological hoopla is going to fool them about the quality of their lives. It didn't then, and it won't now.

Taking stock four years before President Mbeki's presidency comes to an end, what have we?

- We have an emerging, as yet vaguely defined, new redemptive ideology called 'Africanism'.
- We have a crisis of succession as far as the presidency is concerned.
- We have a massive crisis of delivery as far as essential services are concerned.
- We have an emerging ideological fault line beginning to superimpose itself on the crisis of delivery within the ANC: market-driven growth versus populist redistribution.
- We still have predominantly consensual stability in South Africa.
- Consequently we have an active, diverse civil society.
- We do have the human, financial, economic and commercial resources to face most of these challenges.
- We have an electorate increasingly beginning to suffer from ideological fatigue – they want action, no more 'fancy talk' and promises. Apathy is attracting more and more of them.

So, Mr President – good luck! I mean it, and you need it.

MYTHMAKING IN THE NEW SOUTH AFRICA

It has been said that when people define a situation as real, it becomes real in its consequences. When such a situation cannot be corroborated or disproven, and people still persist in defining it as 'real', one has the defining quality of a myth. Most of my public life before 1989 was spent in exposing 'the myth of apartheid'. This 'great lie' was built on a number of 'smaller' myths to sustain it. One of them was the legal attempt to define race in the Population Registration Act. This Act formed the legislative bedrock of all apartheid policies, and permeated the lives of all South Africans down to the most personal, intimate details. For example, Section 16 of the Immorality Act (preventing sex across the 'colour line') and the Prohibition of Mixed Marriages Act depended on the legal definitions of the Population Registration Act.

I became personally involved in helping individuals to be reclassified from 'Coloured to White', from 'White to Coloured' and even from 'Black to Coloured'. Almost without exception the cases had to do with complications around love, marriage and offspring. One occasion that I have written about elsewhere bears repeating, if only to illustrate its significance for the 'new South Africa'. It involved a family by the name of Bodenstein. He came to my house one Sunday afternoon and said he needed my help on a race classification issue. During the 1950s he and his wife-to-be worked on the Blue Train. They decided to marry, but before they could do so the Population Registration Act and the Prohibition of Mixed Marriages Act came onto the statute books. She was classified 'Coloured' and he 'White'. Their love for each other was so strong that they decided to disregard these acts, and got married 'illegally'. When he came to see me he said that they had 24 grandchildren – half classified 'White', the other half 'Coloured'. For the family, Christmas was not a happy time, because the grandchildren would compare notes on education, housing, social services, etc. Could I not help to get his 'Coloured' grandchildren classified as 'White'?

I suggested he get as many as possible of his grandchildren together one evening after my day in Parliament. In a little house in Woodstock, 13 grandchildren and their parents were crowded into a living room. According to the Population Registration Act, Section 5(4)(c), a Coloured is someone – (1) who looks Coloured; (2) whose mother is a Coloured; and (3) who is accepted as Coloured by the Coloured community. I looked at the children and did a quick 5(4)(c) on them, and with dismay thought there was no way I was going to get the 'Coloured' kids to become 'White'. Then to my surprise I was told that those who 'looked' Coloured were actually classified 'White', and the others vice versa.

I went to the relevant cabinet minister, who was Pen Kotze, and told him the solution was simple. If he reclassified the grandmother 'White' all the offspring became

White by definition. If he did not, I would personally see to it that there would be a Bodenstein sob story in the newspapers every weekend. He told me to give him a break, winked, and said he would come back to me. He called me a week later and said he would make half 'White' now, and the rest six months later. If he did them all together at once, it would cause too much of a fuss. And so the Bodenstein family became White and wrote me an effusive letter of thanks.

Today, in the 'New South Africa', they might very well curse me as they are excluded from the benefits of the Broad Based Black Economic Empowerment Act because they are 'White'. If the Bodenstein experience holds any lesson for Whites in the new South Africa it is this: marry a Black so that your children can qualify as beneficiaries of the BBBEEA. However, there is no Population Registration Act that can be manipulated. Your luck is going to depend on some official deciding whether you look Black in order to qualify. In terms of the BBBEEA, 'Black' is a generic term that refers to Coloureds, Asians and Africans, and nowhere is any legal definition given of these terms. There are even some companies who want Chinese to be defined as Black so that they can qualify for 'Empowerment' deals. Imagine Mbeki opening his address to the government of China by saying, 'My dear Black Brethren …'

And so, in the 'New South Africa', the myth of race endures; ask Pallo Jordan, the 'blood' expert. It is one of the enduring legacies of apartheid South Africa, even though many of its other myths have been destroyed.

I started writing this book by saying that the one thing the 'old' and the 'new' South Africa have in common is inventing history, i.e. mythmaking. Not for one second am I suggesting that the myths of the 'new South Africa' are as devastating and destructive in their consequences for human interaction as were the myths of the 'old South Africa'. But they are having far-reaching consequences for policy-making and implementation in trying to meet the challenges of reconstruction in the 'new South Africa'.

Just as FW de Klerk continues to invent himself and the role he played before, during and after the transition from the 'old' to the 'new', so does the ANC leadership:

1 Before transition, during the struggle for liberation, the myth of 'the most titanic army on the African continent' – the ANC, of which Thabo Mbeki was 'a loyal foot soldier'; the myth that within the rank-and-file of the ANC there was/is consensus on the content and meaning of the National Democratic Revolution; this, because 'the leadership' helped 'the masses' to get to the 'correct way' of understanding 'the dynamics of South Africa'; the myth, more by implication than explicitly, that it was 'the exile ANC' that brought 'apartheid to its knees'.

2 During transition, the oft-repeated myth of some 'forceful victory' over the 'apartheid enemy'; the 'crushing of the head of the apartheid snake'; etc.; it was essentially 'a military transition'! Increasingly the average township dweller is asking: If everything is so good, why is everything so bad?

3 Current myths about race, as if 'African', 'Coloured', 'Indian', 'Black', 'White' have self-evident meaning. Just

imagine asking a rural Zulu, Xhosa, Sepedi, Tswana whether a 'Coloured', Indian or Chinese is Black. There is the myth about Black economic liberation 'in general' and African economic liberation 'in particular'; current continental and sub-continental myths about unity of purpose in AU, NEPAD, SADC, PFP and African solidarity in general. The only consensus seems to be that these are wonderful *per diem* watering holes. In South Africa you can be Black but not African, e.g. Coloured and White. In Africa you can be African but not Black, e.g. Mubarak, Gaddafi, Bouteflika, etc. – it doesn't matter, those of us who are Africans have the same 'blood'.

The point about political myths is they need some kind of programmatic infrastructure to keep them going, whether it is Nazi Germany, fascist Italy, a military dictatorship in Chile, democracy in the USA, or communism in the USSR. Eventually myths disappear when the weight of historical pressure and evidence make them irrelevant. Race happens to be one of the most tenacious, enduring myths to survive.

Thomas Kuhn, in his work *The Structure of Scientific Revolutions*, talks about paradigm shifts in a particular discipline, i.e. when new research and evidence becomes so compelling that it challenges the assumptions of a dominant paradigm, and the paradigm shifts or becomes redundant. Over the last 200 years, paradigm shifts in politics have become the order of the day, but especially in the last 50 years.

The programmatic infrastructure that underpinned apartheid has been the subject of endless scrutiny: the laws, homelands, Tricameralism, urban Bantu, etc. etc. When, however, one considers the emerging program-matic infrastructure to underpin the myths of the 'new South Africa', the mind tends to go into free fall.

Firstly, we have a liberal democratic Constitution. As I have said, the defining characteristic of such a Con-stitution is not the celebration of majoritarianism, but constraint on the use and abuse of power. That is why the separation of powers, rule of law, respect for human rights, etc. form such a distinctive part of a liberal democracy. It is true, however, that most 'liberation movements', when they come to power, have a deep distaste for any con-straint on their use, or even abuse, of power. Attempts to circumvent these constraints become the new political game – how is it possible that a movement that epitomises the 'will of the people' and/or 'the masses' can be con-strained in pursuing its mandate? That is why, in a one-dominant-party democracy such as ours, one has to be on the lookout for how key constraining institutions are co-opted, or the executive begins to ignore the legislature or other organs of government. (As I write, 8 December 2005, Xolela Mangcu has tendered his resignation as director of the HSRC citing 'executive interference' in the independence of the organisation.)

Secondly, within a liberal democratic Constitution, another programmatic practice is to centralise decision-making and authoritarian control, euphemistically called democratic centralism. Bluntly put, it means that 'the leadership' of the ruling party controls the party, cabinet, Parliament and all other levels of government. The govern-ment of the USSR made this practice famous. Of course, to pursue a liberal democracy and democratic centralism concurrently is to indulge in serious programmatic contradictions. Something has got to give, and usually it is a liberal democracy.

Thirdly, in order to keep 'the masses' on board, the ideology of a national democratic revolution is propagated. Historically it is almost impossible to find an example where such 'a revolution' has been national, or democratic, or both. The hallmark of such an ideology is the promise of 'large scale', 'fundamental' economic and social redistribution. The promise of 'a chicken in every pot' continues to haunt the ANC. Increasingly the dilemma is that the more they promise, the less the poor and dispossessed are inclined to believe them.

Fourthly, a macro-economic policy referred to as GEAR (Growth, Employment and Redistribution). This is the attempt to use 'the market' as the driver of economic growth and to respond to the challenges of globalisation. Most market economists are enthusiastic in their praise for the success of this policy. Of course, there is a tension between the concurrent pursuit of a national democratic revolution and GEAR. The former promises growth through redistribution; the latter redistribution through growth. The more visible the success of GEAR, the more galling it is to those waiting for delivery from an NDR. The new emerging 'Black' middle class and business elite are a constant reminder of the degree of relative deprivation of 'the masses'. So there we have it! The myths of the 'new South Africa' are maintained by the *concurrent* pursuit of four major programmatic goals: a liberal democracy, democratic centralism, a national democratic revolution, and GEAR. It is like standing on an elevator and trying to walk upstairs and downstairs at the same time. You stay on the same spot, and the world just keeps rolling away from you.

The ANC government is potentially confronted with four paradigm shifts at the same time. In an emerging democracy (*vide* Chile 1973), even one paradigm shift is sufficient to induce some form of authoritarian regression (e.g. Augusto Pinochet). Given the current state of our security forces, the irresolution of the current political leadership and the countervailing sources of influence and power in South Africa, I do not see this as possible in the 'foreseeable future' for South Africa. Who knows? Out of the current confusion, something extraordinarily creative may yet emerge. We remain an amazing society, and given where we have come from I am not without hope for the future. However, whether we are famous or not, and whether we like it or not (and I do not mind at all), most of us are condemned to live on the other side of invented history.

Index